The Australian Defence For think and act in a collaborat the benefits of collaboration a a We space. Collaborative thi

— **Lieutenant-General David Morrison**, *AO, Chief of Army*

If you have been programmed or conditioned by society to believe that success means achieving on your own, you need to realise that no one achieves wealth, happiness, success, long-lasting love or anything else without the guidance and support of others. Innovation starts with collaboration. I can confidently say that I would not be where I am today without consciously working with people who share in my vision and desired outcomes. You are as successful as the people you are surrounded by and Janine has dedicated her whole working life collaborating with and bringing together like-minded people to ensure continued and sustainable success.

— **Layne Beachley**, *seven-time world champion surfer, speaker and author*

Janine gets the challenge, the challenge of getting smart people working together. In *From Me to We* she offers a plan for creating competitive advantage by collaboration.

— **Matt Church**, *author and founder of Thought Leaders Global*

Collaboration is far from a soft skill. It is a bottom-line asset that lifts your team's collective intelligence, increases engagement and drives innovation, providing points of view of risk and opportunities you might otherwise miss.

— **Dan Gregory**, *author and CEO at The Impossible Institute*

Great leaders know that we can do more together than we ever can alone. In today's accelerated and competitive world, building strong relationships that are not only mutually rewarding, but commercially smart, is the new imperative. Garner's book will help you do just that.

— **Margie Warrell**, *best-selling author of* Stop Playing Safe *and* Find Your Courage

What I know is this. When people come together, and they find that place where their ideas and their passions and their values meet — that's where the magic happens. We need to be encouraging more individuals and companies to truly collaborate and land in that place where everybody wins.

— **Emma Isaacs**, *CEO, Business Chicks*

Commercial collaboration is not a 'nice to do' but the key imperative of our times, and holds the only means to solving complex global problems as well as daily business challenges. Commercial collaboration is the smartest way for us to future-proof our world together.

— **Yamini Naidu**, *global thought leader in business storytelling*

In a decentralised, digital and collaborative economy and environment, we will see an increase in commercial collaboration as people try to maintain lean operations while providing more business solutions. Collaboration also has the benefit of scaling up talent and value propositions.

— **Renata Cooper**, *CEO, Forming Circles*

You know you are really collaborating when the question evolves from 'I have this to offer so how big is my slice?' to 'We have all the ingredients, so how big do we want this pie to be?' It takes not only self belief, but also courage and unconditional trust in the talent around you to truly experience fearless and generous collaboration.

— **Paul Walton**, *producer and head of production, Princess Pictures*

Collaboration is about opening up to new possibilities in life by listening, learning and growing; by sharing with inspiring people who lift you higher, and help change your perspectives through sharing knowledge without compromising core beliefs.

— **Louise Agnew**, *principal, LYFE Planning Pty Ltd*

Collaboration is the result of understanding that while knowledge is power, sharing knowledge is empowering.

— **Fiona Craig**, *CEO and founder, Fiona Craig Consulting*

The fusion of talents, skills, knowledge and experience expand the opportunity set of all parties involved in the venture. Whether they are individuals, companies, governments, charities, schools or clubs, the partners to a well-structured and precisely purposed commercial collaboration are likely to derive a range of financial and learning benefits as the miracle of mutuality works its magic.

— **Stuart Findlay**, *executive coach*

We really IS better than me. To be reminded that whatever the circumstances you find yourself in, this outward, others-focused frame will provide clarity and direction for you to create a future you want to be part of with people you love to work with.

— **Rohan Dredge**, *CEO, New Level Leaders*

Collaboration means sharing the gift of yourself to inspire and lift others to a better place.

— **Zahrina Robertson**, *photographer*

For true collaboration you must be open to giving as much as receiving; that is when the real magic happens. Realising the power of true collaboration has put my business on another level.

— **Alicia Beachley**, *CEO, April 5*

Collaboration with people you like, doing the work you like, the way you like is both fulfilling and powerful leverage to commercial success.

— **Christina Guidotti**, *speaker and author of*
How To Have It All

To me, three main things make up collaboration: openness to share (ideas, experience, points of view), leveraging strengths and a commitment to create value from all parties. Collaboration sparks creativity and possibility beyond belief and when done well, produces outcomes and greatness that alone you'd never think was possible.

— **Blythe Rowe**, *founder, Human Incite*

When you are working within a Me environment, ultimately you are working under the belief that you are the only person with any real ideas of worth. True success comes in the understanding that team ideas drive a business to its peak — when 'We' achieve the dream.

— **Kate Stone**, *CEO, typecast*

Collaboration is when you've genuinely got someone's back and they've got yours.

— **Michelle Sutherland**, *employee engagement manager,*
Hewlett Packard

FROM

ME
TO
WE

Why **commercial collaboration** will future-proof
business, leaders and personal success

JANINE GARNER

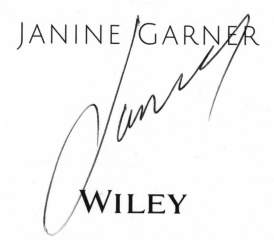

WILEY

First published in 2015 by John Wiley & Sons Australia, Ltd
42 McDougall St, Milton Qld 4064

Office also in Melbourne

Typeset in 11/13 pt Minion Pro

© Curious Minds Pty Ltd 2015

The moral rights of the author have been asserted

Author:	Garner, Janine, author.
Title:	From Me to We: Why commercial collaboration will future-proof business, leaders and personal success / Janine Garner.
ISBN:	9780730318491 (pbk.)
	9780730318507 (ebook)
Notes:	Includes index.
Subjects:	Business networks.
	Strategic alliances (Business).
	Strategic planning.
	Organisational effectiveness.
Dewey Number:	658.4012

Cover design by Wiley

Cover and internal image: © iStock.com/donatas1205

Illustrations by James Henderson

Printed in Singapore by C.O.S. Printers Pte Ltd

10 9 8 7 6 5 4 3 2 1

Disclaimer

The material in this publication is of the nature of general comment only, and neither purports nor intends to be advice. Readers should not act on the basis of any matter in this publication without considering (and if appropriate, taking) professional advice with due regard to their own particular circumstances. The author and publisher expressly disclaim all and any liability to any person, whether a purchaser of this publication or not, in respect of anything and of the consequences of anything done or omitted to be done by any such person in reliance, whether whole or partial, upon the whole or any part of the contents of this publication.

Contents

About the author

Janine Garner is passionate about commercial collaboration, driving courageous conversations, influential leadership and, above all, future-proofing business.

She is the founder and CEO of the LBDGroup, a community of successful and results-oriented businesswomen and entrepreneurs working collaboratively to drive continued change and success.

Janine is also the founder of Australia's first gift-giving circle, First Seeds Fund, which is committed to supporting Australian women and children in education and employment.

She has won an International Stevie Award, has been voted one of the Top 10 DARE Devil Women of 2013 by *DARE* magazine, is listed in 2013 as one of Australia's 'Most Inspiring Women' by *Madison* magazine and has been nominated for the Telstra Businesswomen Awards.

Janine is a sought-after keynote speaker, mentor and business adviser. She writes every week for her own blog and is a regular commentator in business print and online media.

Acknowledgements

This book is a working example of the power of commercial collaboration and the improved thinking that emerges when collective intelligence is engaged: mentors, business colleagues, other experts, friends and family have all been a diverse and amazing group of people that inspire me, mentor me, support my dream, provide incredible friendship and, critically, keep me sane. This journey, my first foray into writing, will forever be a journey I cherish — I have learned so much about myself and, most importantly, how you can achieve so much more than you ever thought you were capable of if your why is strong enough.

I would like to first of all thank my children — Flynn, Taya and Carter. You are all an inspiration to me every day, showing me that opportunity is everywhere and teaching me to open my eyes and ears to the gifts that surround us. Flynn, your wisdom and empathy will take you far; Taya, the joy and happiness you bring to life every day is infectious; and Carter, your hunger for life and determination to be the best is incredible. Thank you to my 'babies' for supporting my dream and your patience on the evenings and weekends when sport and playtime were missed because I had to lock myself away and focus on 'Mummy's book'. I love you all up to the sky and back and I am so proud of everything you already are and everything you are destined to become.

Thank you to my gorgeous husband, Jason. You are my rock, my support, my encourager and my believer all rolled into one. Without you I would not have had the courage to take ownership of my dream and without your continued support, encouragement and love (as well as having to pick up the majority of the family demands while I was writing this book)

I would not be where I am today. You are my soul mate and always will be. I am all I am and more now because of you and the family we have together. May our dreams continue to get bigger.

Thank you to Jen Daillitz and Abigail Disney for providing my lollipop moments, igniting the spirit and inspiring me to take ownership of my own journey.

Matt Church, thank you for your patience, encouragement and above all for pushing me to become more. I have loved every debate, conversation and challenge set — you have stretched my thinking and pushed me to the edge of my comfort zone. You have been and will continue to be my mentor and teacher, and your willingness to share your knowledge, insight and guidance to help others achieve what you see in them is collaboration in action every day.

To the team at Wiley — your support, advice and guidance has been amazing from the get go. Particular thanks go to Lucy and Allison. I loved every meeting, email conversation and phone call, and with your input and investment this book has become so much more.

To all the friends that keep me sane. The kids — Louise, Maria, Gell, Caroline, Heidi and Janey — we may be dispersed throughout the world but the friendship, love and support that was cemented 25 years ago and the experiences we have all been through have shaped me to become who I am. I value your love and friendship always. To Andy and Maria for dreaming with me and for helping shape our Aussie life and to Sarah, Shannon and Julie for helping me keep things on track and in perspective.

To my fellow game changers, the contributors in this book and to all the members of the LBDGroup, thank you for your encouragement, support and belief in the journey. For contributing and collaborating and becoming part of a community that is creating ripples of change. Each of you are shaping the future of business, of generations, of leadership, and proving that together we can become so much more.

A special thank you to WW — you know who you are. You are an inspiration. Your ongoing strength and resilience inspires me and all who are lucky enough to know you. Your continuous encouragement and quiet involvement in helping to build my vision and big-picture dream is so appreciated. Thank you for all your support through the laughter and tears, the virtual horse races and the 'my little pony' moments. Without this the late nights and early mornings of writing would have been so much harder. Your guidance, friendship and love are something I will forever value.

And finally thank you to you the reader for taking the time to read this book and exploring a more collaborative way of working — a way that embraces diversity, values differences and sees the opportunity and increased sum of collective intelligence.

Introduction

> Coming together is a beginning; keeping together is progress; working together is success.
>
> — *Henry Ford, businessman*

What does collaboration mean to you?

Are you aware that commercial collaboration is the key to endless opportunities to future-proof your business, your career and your own success?

Great potential can be created when you move from being solely focused on Me — *my* skills, *my* job, *my* business, *my* leadership challenges — to working freely in a world of We, where there is active collaboration and sharing of knowledge, insight and intellect. Where you openly talk about failures, and equally share knowledge; where honesty, integrity and a belief in opportunity and possibility can create the freedom to invent, to innovate and to disrupt the status quo and, ultimately, to future-proof yourself.

Sounds easy, doesn't it? Well, if this is the case, why aren't more people doing it? Why hasn't commercial collaboration become the business norm? Why do we continue to feel that that the only way to deliver results, profits and performance is to do it ourselves? We continue to find it challenging to actively open doors for someone else to achieve success and to expect nothing in return. The automatic operating system for many is one of 'I must protect myself', 'I must not share my thoughts or ideas', 'the competition is out to get me' and, finally — 'I know best'.

This is not the mindset for commercial collaboration. To collaborate commercially is *not* about:

- the close-minded, protective, 'take, take, take' of ideas and intellectual property from others
- the business card swap-fest associated with traditional networking events
- survival of the self (or even of the fittest).

My corporate journey is not uncommon — I worked like a maniac to get to where I thought I wanted to be, where I thought I *should* be: at the top of a highly coveted corporate sector. I do not discount the journey, or the thrill of making it to the pinnacle. What I found when I got there, however, was that although the spirit for commercial collaboration may have been present ... as the old saying goes, the corporate flesh was weak. There were times when I felt we had some brilliant flashes of team thought and engagement, but unfortunately they weren't sustained.

So, three years ago I came to a realisation. If I wanted to surround myself with the kind of thought leadership, diversity, knowledge and idea sharing that I knew was needed in commercial life, I had to strike out on my own. This was how the LBDGroup was born. There was a niche for a community of like-minded, results-oriented businesswomen who wanted to interact commercially at a level that wasn't currently available — either within their own corporations, or with other entrepreneurs in their own sectors.

LBDGroup is unique. This is not only my opinion. The cross-pollination of ideas, IP, talent, leadership, thought and values is honestly something that I cannot put into words. The interaction and exchange of cutting-edge innovation, both in terms of the intangible and the tangible, is something that the businesspeople involved are actively embracing as they connect, collaborate and contribute to drive innovative thinking, new solutions and strategies to secure their careers and business futures.

The level of commercial collaboration that has resulted from this community has proven very clearly the essential points of this book: when one turns from the solitary space of Me, as satisfying as it may feel at the time, to the collaborative space of We, the benefits it brings are overwhelmingly positive and lead to that amazing lightness that only comes with future-proofing one's career and success path.

The heartbeat of commercial collaboration is understanding and appreciating the change that is needed to future-proof businesses, careers and leaders. It is a new operating system that requires an equally new set of skills. It needs courage and a willingness to be authentic. It requires us to disrupt current norms, to proactively collaborate to drive change — and it will not occur in a vacuum.

Commercial collaboration is putting into practice Aristotle's philosophy that 'the whole is greater than the sum of the parts'. When in balance, working together serves a greater purpose. Ultimately it will drive you, your business and your potential to heights that you never imagined possible — and probably would not achieve if you continued to go it alone.

Imagine a different world. One where:

- we are inspired and encouraged to openly share thoughts, opinions and knowledge
- working environments respect the needs of the 'whole' employee
- individuals can thrive on the freedom to create, to explore, to be curious about new possibilities
- workers can add value and contribute to the big-picture goals
- leaders are authentic and honest
- we are constantly learning and evolving as a result of embracing diversity of position, thought, gender and age
- we embrace uniqueness

- we respect each other's visions and dreams
- we create actions that drive continued success for each other
- we create space for people to share their amazingness
- we have the courage to lead, to share and equally to ask for help
- we appreciate the human in people as much as the financial return and the big-picture vision
- there is no political game-playing, no saying one thing and doing another, no abuse of power that protects position, self, ego
- collaboration is valued strategically and aligned positively to continued growth, evolution, creative thinking and future-proofing for all.

So what to do? The answer is simple.

Collaborate.

Talk.

Engage.

And, most importantly, find a way to stop being all about 'me, me, me' and looking inward for answers that simply aren't there. Find a way to turn with confidence and openness from Me to We, to working collaboratively.

The barriers between genders, between generations, between cultures, between the inventors and the investors, between the change-makers, the visionaries and those that make it happen — these all have to be broken down. This is all a part of the evolution of Me to We. This is all a part of collaborative business.

To collaborate is to lead. To lead with inspiration, and gusto, and innovation and heart.

This book is essentially about *why* a new operating system is needed, and *how* to move from Me to We and collaborate commercially. It will break down the nine essential steps to enable you to answer 'What do we need to do?' and then examine and explain the seven ReConnect Principles leaders and businesses will need to adopt to collaboratively reconnect and do what they do best: survive, thrive and future-proof their success. The ReConnect Principles are:

1 Be brave

2 Build a diverse network

3 Full disclosure

4 Disrupt

5 Exchange value

6 Think bigger

7 Sponsor others.

> *We need to develop and disseminate an entirely new paradigm and practice of collaboration that supersedes the traditional silos that have divided governments, philanthropists and private enterprises for decades and replace it with networks of partnerships working together to create a globally prosperous society.*
>
> — Simon Mainwaring, CEO, We First Inc.

Part I

When I was young and free and my imagination had no limits, I dreamed of changing the world. As I grew older and wiser I discovered the world would not change so I shortened my sights and decided to change only my country. But it too seemed immovable. As I grew into my twilight years, in one last desperate attempt, I settled for changing my family — those closest to me — but alas they would have none of it. And now as I lie on my deathbed I suddenly realise if I had only changed myself first then by example I would have changed my family. From their inspiration and encouragement I would have been able to better my country and who knows I may have even changed the world.

— *Words found written on the tomb of an Anglican Bishop*
in Westminster Abbey

chapter 1

There's an evolution going on

> Every successful organisation has to make the transition from a world defined primarily by repetition to one primarily defined by change. This is the biggest transformation in the structure of how humans work together since the Agricultural Revolution.
>
> — *Bill Drayton, CEO and founder of ASHOKA*

Anybody who believes that the business landscape is the same as it was in the 'old days' has their head well and truly buried in the 20th-century sand. There is an evolution going on that is affecting the business world and how we lead and manage within it.

We are all being forced to rethink how we behave and what we do. The changes of greater society — changes in generations, gender dynamics and technology — are leading to a shift in business from large, highly structured corporate entities to agile, innovative entrepreneurial enterprises.

This evolution isn't about to stop any time soon — if anything, the pace of change is only going to increase exponentially — and it is challenging us to rethink what we do, how we communicate with each other and how we will operate as leaders and businesses into the future. It is challenging us to develop new operating systems to future-proof success. It is challenging us, as managers, to learn to lead movements in a way that makes our teams secure enough to think and act collaboratively.

As leaders, business owners and individuals, we are caught between two worlds: one that thrives on volatility and one that craves stability. There is an ongoing tug of war between the pursuit of growth on one side and a desire for control and constancy on the other. In the pursuit of growth, we actively seek knowledge and experience, looking to others for inspiration and ideas, creating big-picture visions for our future self. On the opposite side of the tug of war is the need for control: our existing work streams and structures prefer predictability, productivity and control.

The evolution is making:

- leadership styles change from 'tell' to 'engage', with leadership now about inspiring and becoming truly authentic

- traditional business structures far more fluid and blended

- innovation and invention essential business tools as consumers want better products and services delivered more quickly than ever before

- agility and decisiveness prerequisites in our teams and in our leadership.

In this chapter, we will explore the current business landscape, and how a collaborative approach is integral to surviving and thriving into the future.

The world where you live

The future is so uncertain that many organisations and consultants have adopted a term originally coined by the US Army to describe the results of the end of the Cold War — the acronym VUCA. VUCA describes a world that is increasingly Volatile, Uncertain, Complex and Ambiguous. This world is fast, change-focused and demanding. Agile thinking, decision-making and action are now the norm.

And the result? Individuals and leaders are left feeling alone, exhausted and uncertain about their place in the future. The rapid changes that are taking place are affecting how we operate. We are forced into the space of Me — one where we reassess, consider options, invest and focus on the self. We protect what we know, learn what we don't and then hope that we can fake it till we make it.

The collaborative economy

So what approaches will work in our rapidly changing environment? The collaborative economy is where networks of connected individuals, communities and businesses — as opposed to centralised closed-door thinking and business planning — work together to drive success. The power of this is inestimable as it connects people, businesses, skills, services, products and space to drive new opportunities and strategies for future-proofing. Who could have imagined, for example, that one day — and that day is now — NASA would be using LEGO building blocks to educate astronauts in the International Space Station, and in turn providing LEGO with inspiration for their designs? Or that Coca-Cola would be working with ECO Plastics to develop sustainable and ethical bottles? Their agreement marks a turning point in the processing of industrial waste in the UK.

Collaboration is so much more than the sum of its parts. The nuts and bolts of sending an email, being on social media, placing a paid advertisement or doing a mass mailing are no longer enough in terms of 'engagement'. What consumers and internal clients are asking for is that businesses understand them; that they speak to them as human beings, not numbers. They are demanding a customer-centric approach to decision-making and new product development. They want to know the depth behind the logo, the thinking and the rationale behind the leadership.

The collaborative economy is a space where if we are authentic, play by rules of openness and transparency, and follow our passions, we have the opportunity to build collective intelligence, trust and connection, and to surprise and influence many.

Future uncertainty

The phenomenal speed of change that got us to the 21st century's technological frenzy is not going to slow down any time soon — and it is creating an uncertain future on a global business level. In *The World Is Flat*, Thomas Friedman suggests that the changes that we are experiencing now are 'directly or indirectly touching a lot more people on the planet' than ever before. In an increasingly decentralised and digitally connected economy, companies and people need to constantly explore ways to improve — and if they don't, what is the risk? Fall behind. Lose momentum. Flatline. Fail.

The future is uncertain for the following reasons:

- A worldwide unstable economic environment continues to place increasing pressure on governments, businesses and individuals.
- The changing political structures around the world affect consumer confidence and stability.
- Evolving social trends and behaviours are influencing the individual needs of society and the labour force.
- The growth of entrepreneurialism and more agile, fast-moving, disruptive businesses is challenging the traditional corporate structures, growth strategies and decision-making.

Figure 1.1 shows that we are at the juncture of three distinct areas of uncertainty: innovation, socio-economic dynamics and business change. These three critical areas are summarised on pages 8 and 9 and will be covered in more detail in chapter 2.

Figure 1.1: the future is uncertain

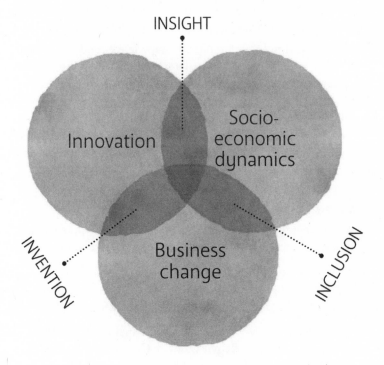

Innovation

We are living in a highly connected world where information and resources are readily available 24/7. This access to information is supporting consumer awareness and self-education, and enabling research and ongoing improvements to products, communication methods and delivery solutions. In the 'old' world, intelligent thinking, high-quality products, services and the breadth of range that is available now simply didn't exist. Consumers would do their research, find what they want and make a purchase. Now everything is everywhere in mass supply and we want it better, quicker and cheaper.

Increased technology, increased knowledge and economic instability — all of these are driving a demand for innovation on a continuous basis for large and small businesses alike. The entrepreneur is everywhere; new businesses are born and new products created overnight. Evolution is essential for survival, for economic viability, for customer engagement, and most importantly, to keep staff engaged and secure in the knowledge that our business is where they want to be working.

Socio-economic dynamics

Economic changes, changing family structures and globalisation have altered society forever. The main changing dynamics are:

- *the role of women in the workforce.* More women are entering higher education, participating in the workforce and becoming increasingly wealthy than ever before.

- *generational change.* We are experiencing four generations of people at work — Baby Boomers, Gen X, Gen Y and Gen Z. Each generation is bringing to the workplace a pre-determined set of values, work ethic and career expectations.

- *work-life balance.* The work-life balance debate is evolving as more people are talking about creating balanced lives.

Business change

While some industries and corporate environments remain more rigid than others, there is no doubting that both business etiquette and the 'rules of engagement' have moved on. It may not be as rapidly as some of us would like, but nonetheless, the goalposts — and the goals — of modern leaders are shifting. And only for the better.

Business processes, structures and operations are evolving at a much faster pace than ever before in an effort to keep ahead of change while future-proofing business. Consumers are becoming increasingly vocal about their expectations. The fight is on to find talented and skilled employees. Competition for products, sales, profit and people is now global. Two of the areas business is changing in are as follows:

- *The make-up of our future workforce.* Jobs that are secure today may not even exist in the future as they are replaced by technology or outsourced to other areas in the world. Equally, who knows what jobs may exist in the future given the speed of change that we are witnessing?

- *The ubiquity of entrepreneurship.* Many economists believe that the growing trend across the world towards entrepreneurship will drive economic and financial stability over the coming years. The impact of small business cannot go unnoticed as it continues to be the incubator for innovation and employment.

The Me to We shift

The question being asked by many in this VUCA world is 'What do I have to do next?' These rapid changes are demanding a new operating system — one where we can bring our skills, strengths and talents to the table and together amplify and share expertise to create progressive, results-oriented solutions.

As shown in figure 1.1 (see p. 7), the sweet spot of opportunity is at the juncture of innovation, socio-economic dynamics and business change. It is a place where things happen differently, creative thinking is accepted and disruption and innovation are the norm. A place where commercial collaboration drives change and shifts results. This juncture requires a shift from Me to We; it asks us to jump with both feet into the space of commercial collaboration.

Commercial collaboration is the key to future-proofing business, leadership, careers and success. The uncertain future is demanding us to work together, engaging intellect and insight from diverse inputs, disrupting the way things have been to thrive in the ever-evolving future space.

Figure 1.2 illustrates the journey from status quo to leveraging and leading, to future-proofing success through commercial collaboration.

The status quo is the enemy

The status quo is the enemy of change, new ideas, innovation and invention. The status quo is not a friend of commercial collaboration, and stepping out of it is the first step of moving from Me to We.

Change resisters risk falling behind the competition. Accepting the status quo, resisting change and refusing to explore alternate thinking and solutions results in complacency and the risk of failure in an uncertain future. In fact, it is my belief that those that are happy with the status quo will see no progress; they will flatline and eventually decline in performance.

The high achievers refuse to accept the status quo; they evolve and align opportunity for themselves and their businesses with the opportunities around them — and they do this all the time; they are restless.

As Thomas Edison said, 'Opportunity is missed by most people because it is dressed in overalls and looks a lot like work.'

Figure 1.2: commercial collaboration is the key

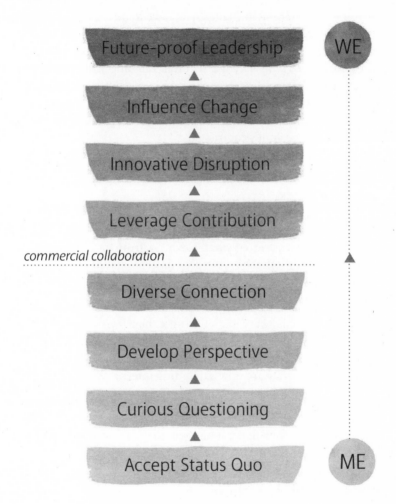

It starts with a question

Questioning the status quo opens up a world of opportunity. It's the catalyst for change that can alter your outcome and help you become an inventor and explore the possibilities. Always assume there is another way.

If you want anything to change, you have to be the one to make it happen. Changing the status quo requires questioning to understand the current situation and to seek ways to improve the present. Driving change requires ongoing exploration of what could be and active inquiry into the options available. Without questioning and exploration, doors to the future are slammed firmly shut, the lens of opportunity becomes blurred and thinking becomes contracted.

The power of questioning is illustrated with the following examples:

- McDonald's was born when Ray Kroc asked the question, 'Why can't I get a good hamburger at the side of the road?'
- Instagram was created when Kevin Systrom and Mike Krieger questioned how images could be shared on smartphones.
- Jodie Fox questioned why, if men could get customised suits from Asia, women couldn't get their own shoe designs in the same way. With business partners Michael Fox and Mike Knapp she created Shoes of Prey to provide just that service, and they are now expanding internationally.

One thing is certain. Many successful individuals do not become successful by sitting in the status quo waiting for success to come to them. They make it happen, they are curious — and it all starts with a question.

Perspective is a choice

Questioning leads to a new perspective. This in turn presents a choice. Are you going to choose to have a wide perspective on your future or limit your thinking?

A new perspective opens up new possibilities: opportunities as well as risks. It kick-starts the internal drive to move away from the status quo to a new future. For the individual this could be exploring new skill sets, training opportunities or career choices. For a business it could be new product development, new distribution channels, new services or new solutions to existing problems.

For example, who would have imagined that anyone, anywhere, could monetise a spare room to travellers? Yet in just six years Airbnb has moved to the forefront of the collaborative economy, building a community marketplace featuring more than 600 000 listings in 192 countries. It is a collaboration between entrepreneurs, an oversupply of product availability and consumers matching the supply with an ever-increasing demand.

A 2012 *Harvard Business Review* report, 'Train Your People to Take Others' Perspectives', shares that 'successful collaboration between stakeholders starts with what social psychologists call perspective taking: the ability to see the world through someone else's eyes'. Developing a new perspective and choosing to enable change is crucial for development and evolution. It's about opening yourself to what is happening around you, being curious about solutions and exploring possibilities.

Connection: Safe or diverse?

Perspective brings new connections, and the more diverse the connections the more opportunities can be leveraged.

It's part of human nature to seek out like-minded people as we search for further growth and development. But if we only connect with people exactly like ourselves, from the same industries, with the same skills and knowledge, this can lead us right back to sitting in the status quo.

In the report 'Managing Yourself : A Smarter Way to Network', *Harvard Business Review* found that the difference between the top 20 per cent of successful executives and the rest was that they ensure the network they connect with is diverse. It was found that these diverse networks consisting of people from different backgrounds, industries and skill bases created new discussion and insight into problems and encouraged open and creative thinking.

Connecting with a diverse network requires confidence in your expertise and value. It requires courage to actively speak up, debate and share and it pulls on vulnerability: the ability to share openly what you don't know.

Leveraged contribution

Building the right connections and contributing to each other's success leverages opportunity for all. Connecting with others is only the start of commercial collaboration — the next step is one of contribution.

Contribution only happens with a willingness to openly share knowledge and insight and to being risk tolerant and open to challenge, new ideas and opportunities. Contribution is not simply about sharing a business card, or sitting at a networking event or business meeting and saying nothing.

Commercial collaboration happens when courage and bravery kick in. When you connect, and with honesty and, to some extent, vulnerability, share your own ideas, insights and failures with the aim of adding value to others.

Leverage happens when there is an authentic desire to improve the positions and opportunities for others. It is about openly sharing your expertise — with no expectation of anything in return — combined with honesty about what you don't know and a willingness to listen to possible solutions and advice.

Disruption

Contribution leads to disruption — the next step on the ladder in figure 1.2 (see p. 11). Disruption happens because change has to happen. Disruption creates a shift in thinking, drives innovation and changes behaviour.

When disruption happens, it does the following:

- displaces existing methods, markets and technologies
- invents something new and more efficient
- uncovers a previously untapped market or solution to a problem
- drives intrigue, interest and trial by new adopters.

Those who choose to collaborate to drive commercial success are the ones who drive disruption.

Influence is magic in action

Without influence change cannot occur. The opportunity to build trust and influence, one to one and many to many, has never before been so accessible. Social media and the internet have created a platform of influence on a significant scale.

Once connection, contribution and disruption create results, others notice. This is when businesses and individuals become known as change-makers; they have the ability to influence many. They are capable of more than they ever were on their own, operating outside of the safety zone of protecting themselves to contributing to new ideas and solutions as part of a larger community of We thinkers with a high-growth mindset.

Future-proof and lead

Future-proofing ourselves and our businesses requires a new operating system — one of commercial collaboration to actively engage, connect and share with others to drive mutual success.

Commercial collaboration requires people to move from a place of Me to a collaborative place of We. Collaboration:

- creates momentum
- drives new thinking

- builds resilience and determination to succeed
- enables individuals and businesses to explore possibilities and develop strategies to future-proof success.

This is not about a revolution; it's about evolution. If your company makes glass jars, it's not about suddenly stopping making glass jars and starting making shoes. It's about questioning your current position, exploring the best possible way to make glass jars that engages and involves your people, and considering what you need to do to disrupt the status quo and move forward. It's about giving your team a voice in your methods, collaborating and being open to conversation and advice, and creating the freedom to think, debate, create and invent.

A challenge for big corporates? Absolutely. Unattainable? Absolutely not.

As leaders, we need to be the ones motivating and guiding, the ones disrupting and thinking differently. We are the ones to whom others are looking for inspiration. We must always be on the lookout for potential new ways of doing business — we must be prepared to test different approaches. And any approach must involve every member of our companies.

Are you willing to step into the We space and be noticed? Are you prepared to contribute more than you think you are capable of? Are you ready to change the rules and step out from the expected masses?

There's an evolution going on. Make yourself a part of it. Be willing to instigate change, to give yourself and your team a common purpose — a say in what they are striving towards. Because it's the way not just of the business future, but of the present.

Summary

> The world today is volatile, uncertain, complex and ambiguous, with ever-increasing amounts of information creating the need for commercial collaboration.

> We are at the juncture of three distinct areas of uncertainty: innovation, socio-economic dynamics and business. A shift from Me to We is critical to future-proof business, careers and success.

> Opportunity will come from questioning the status quo, developing new perspectives, connecting with and contributing to others, exploring ways to disrupt the norm and influence others.

> Commercial collaboration drives influence, innovation and invention.

chapter 2

Change is opportunity

The reasonable man adapts himself to the world; the unreasonable one persists in trying to adapt the world to himself. Therefore all progress depends on the unreasonable man.

— *George Bernard Shaw, playwright*

The evolution that we are witnessing in society — and, more specifically, business society — is naturally demanding change. There is an ongoing war between the need for stability and the need for growth. It is up to each of us, as leaders and business owners, to actively listen to the demands of this society and evolve how we operate accordingly so that what we do aligns with — and leads — the new paradigm.

We live in a highly connected world. The constant transformations happening on both a domestic and global level are affecting each of us as we try to maintain balance in our personal lives while striving for our dreams. Business is also under pressure as evolution within society demands constant innovation and invention in product design, delivery, communication, marketing and customer service, and in business itself, from office layouts to organisational structures, from leadership styles and culture to working hours and communication platforms.

Societal evolution is driving the general feeling of uncertainty about what the future will hold — especially for Gen X and the

Baby Boomers, who have had certainties stripped away over the past decade, both financially and philosophically. For these two generations in particular, who make up the majority of the leadership pool at present, this feeling of the unknown is resulting in business methodology regression.

Regression to what? To the comfort of the known. To the self. To the safe space of Me, when what is actually needed is courage, confidence and the bravery to move to the We space of commercial collaboration, which will enable them to create the solutions needed to future-proof their own and their team's successes.

The three critical areas driving change are:

- consumers' desire for continued innovation and invention
- global socio-economic evolution
- business practices and procedures.

Unless and until these drivers are actively addressed, change cannot be effectively managed, the balance between stability and growth will teeter constantly, and regression to the space of Me will continue. The three areas of the model will now be discussed.

All hail the inventors, the innovators, the game changers

We are in the midst of one of the biggest innovation revolutions in the history of mankind.

— Guy Krige, associate director, PwC

We all want instant gratification. 'Smart' technology has created an almost artificial urgency to invent, to create, to meet and exceed demands and to change the game at a faster pace than ever before. We now have to find solutions to problems that we didn't even know existed and to explore what exists outside the safety zone. To innovate.

There is no question that innovation is a catalyst for change, and is one of the most powerful ways to drive business growth in today's ultra-competitive and ever-changing environment. Every new development feels like a major turning point and involves incredible amounts of research and testing, but all it does is drive the need for further innovation.

Brands and businesses have no choice; it's a case of recreate, rejuvenate, reinvent — or retrench. Consumers have control. They are more educated than ever before, and they have so much choice as to where to spend their money. In an increasingly straitened global economic climate, this is of massive importance. What consumers want is innovation and invention, solutions to problems — and they want them now. They want improvements, modifications and more functionality on things that to all intents and purposes are already working. And when the innovation is in place, they want increased speed to market and engagement from the offerer through interesting, unique, never-before-seen advertising and publicity campaigns, value adds, promotions and exclusivity.

So what is the reality for business leaders? Enormous pressure.

Ideas have to become actions quickly, effectively and profitably. Decisions *must* be made. The demand for speed of production has in turn become a product in itself. Delivery has become just as important as the innovation. Any business that doesn't treat production as a priority is immediately going to fall behind. This may be due to a failure on the part of its leaders to:

- listen and respond to consumer demand
- understand the constant need to innovate and do it with speed and impact
- treat production with respect.

Innovation and its delivery have become the ultimate keys to competitive advantage.

Much like production as a product, the advent of the internet as a branding tool, with social media marketing, e-commerce and multimedia platforms for communications in use 24/7, is throwing the rules of economic engagement out the window. A brand can make or break it in a megabyte because the internet drives marketing by virtual word of mouth like a virus on steroids. If your innovation is the equivalent of an iPhone? Magic. A BlackBerry? You may want to start looking for new investors. Under a new company name, of course.

It's a simple equation for 21st-century business, and thus for 21st-century leaders:

Innovation + Decision + Teamwork = Advantage

Innovative businesses embed an iterative approach to innovation throughout their organisations. Large companies are allocating more time, money and resources to specialist research and development (R&D) programs. New job titles have emerged as specific 'innovation' departments are established with the sole responsibility of pioneering solutions to systems, processes, product delivery, market communication and new product development. Ideation workshops, innovation away days, brainstorms and blue skies are all gaining popularity. And while small- to medium-sized companies don't necessarily have the resources to put aside for specific departments focused purely on innovation, there is a general consensus that innovative thinking is the key to success.

Innovation is multidimensional, and is apparent in these areas:

- delivery
- distribution
- products
- communication.

Delivery

The digital revolution has created the need for instant gratification, and the more innovative the means of delivery, the more likely the engagement. Speed is a necessity; two weeks' delivery used to be the norm, and now it's free same-day delivery combined with free return policies. We ask for a bank loan or an insurance quote online and expect an immediate answer. We search for information and get frustrated when we can't find it at the end of our fingertips. We want information in writing, audio, video, 140-character tweets and texts. The expectation is that we can get whatever we want by any means available to us and whenever we want. The challenge for leaders is to constantly find new ways to deliver solutions — quicker, better, more efficiently and at an acceptable price point.

In 2007, in response to growing music piracy, Radiohead launched its album *In Rainbows* itself, allowing its fan base to pay as much or as little as it wanted and to download directly from the band's website. In a letter to *NME* magazine, the lead singer of U2, Bono, said Radiohead had 'been courageous and imaginative trying to figure out some new relationship with their audience'. It was a gamble, but it was a calculated gamble because, realistically, Radiohead's fan base could have downloaded it before it was even legally released. This way at least, the band was showing faith in its audience and a willingness to set up a value exchange with them, while offering the same convenient delivery they would get if they downloaded it illegally. This was collaborative business.

Distribution

Multichannel distribution has become the norm and is evolving at break-neck speed. The trusted door-to-door salesman of the 1940s has been replaced by anonymous online purchasing with products available from anywhere in the world at the click of a button. E-commerce is growing at an exponential speed. According to eMarketer's latest forecasts, worldwide business-to-consumer e-commerce sales will increase by 20.1 per cent in 2014 to reach $1.5 trillion, with growth coming predominantly from emerging markets. Collaborative consumption is growing as consumers rent, lease or share goods instead of buying. What this means for business leaders is a need to secure the best online customer service agents and technical staff to keep existing and potential customers satisfied with their online experience.

Products

Everyone wants better products. More functionality. New technologies. New solutions, even if they are completely superfluous. Everyone is looking for the next big thing; it seems as though the entire globe is being driven by the FOMO (fear of missing out) phenomenon. In 2013 alone, Apple's R&D costs were reported to be US$4.5 billion, with its executives believing that focused investment in R&D is critical to securing its competitive position in the marketplace. R&D consists of no longer two neglected workers in the basement, and effective leaders ignore it at their peril.

Communication

No longer is communication confined to pen and paper. We can communicate via writing and voice, on paper, digitally and on video — a group of 50 can have a virtual meeting if desired. The ways in which brands can communicate has grown exponentially as they attempt to engage via multiple platforms, tapping into all the senses through word, sound, smell, and visual and hands-on experiences.

Marketing messages reach us via email, social media, text and snail mail — popping up more and more when we least expect them, pre-empting our behaviours, and influencing our thinking and spending, based on the data mined from our previous activity. And we respond by purchasing, when the message and the product align with our needs, which is increasingly common.

We expect brands and business to know us, and we are demanding innovations that deliver relevant messaging. Brands that are trusted are able to aggregate like-minded content, and users trust these sources of knowledge: we have witnessed bloggers sharing aggregated merchandise solutions, thought leaders propagating each other's content, and crowdsourcing delivering unique products with guaranteed sales funnels established prior to launch.

The communication methods of the 21st century and the ability to reach millions create powerful systems to facilitate mobility of message, product and service. In turn, leaders who are innovating are investing in technology capable of providing this type of systemic reach. The outlay is worth it.

Information overload

Thanks to the likes of Google and Wikipedia our knowledge base is growing exponentially, contributing to the speed of change for both ourselves and our environment.

There are frightening statistics about the number of marketing messages bombarding us every day. According to author and marketing strategy consultant Andrew Szabo, in 1970, the average person was exposed to about five hundred advertisements each day. In the early 1990s, it was 5000. Today the often-quoted statistic is *30 000*. Whether it is 5000 or 50 000, the reality is that there is an enormous amount of white noise that we, on a daily basis, are wading through. Darren Hardy, publisher of *SUCCESS* magazine, shared in his 8 March 2011 editor's letter that by the 1900s it had taken 150 years to double human knowledge. Fast track to the year 2020, and the predictions are that it will only take *72 days* to double knowledge. Imagine the increased complexity of information in the future, and the challenges in trying to distil and identify opportunity — we find it difficult enough now.

Socio-economic upheaval

There are three dimensions of socio-economic change affecting the journey from Me to We:

- the role of women in society
- generational change
- work-life balance demands.

The increasing influence of women

Smart organisations — and those that succeed over the next decade and beyond — will understand that the twenty-first century is the 'Women's Century'. In the years ahead, women's economic participation and entrepreneurial growth will drive the world's economy. It's no longer a matter of 'if' but of 'to what heights'.

— Muhtar Kent, chairman of the board and CEO, Coca-Cola

Women are the spending power of more than two-thirds of Australian households. They represent just under half the global population and are the fastest growing group of consumers worldwide. They not only make up a significant portion of the workforce, they are rapidly becoming the fastest-growing entrepreneurial group in both the first and third worlds. Women who work, whether it is on an executive level or in a cottage industry, are building a new society. They have created a new paradigm as they outsource and create virtual networks to enable them to follow their own dreams of success and achieve 'balance': everything from child care to ironing, personal administration and household chores is subcontracted to allow the hours traditionally spent on these tasks to be invested in their own personal goals.

For the first time in history, an increasing number of women are becoming independently (and openly) wealthy. We are seeing a significant shift in financial and personal power as the numbers of women not only at work but in positions of influence continue to grow.

The shift that this is driving in society cannot be ignored. In her book *The XX Factor*, Alison Wolf discussed the phenomenon of female independence: 'Millions of women born from the mid-20th century on can support themselves comfortably, make serious careers, start their own businesses and, indeed, raise children alone.'

In the UK, the Office of National Statistics predicts that by the year 2020 women's pay will overtake men's. Forty-six per cent of millionaires are women. Women now own 48 per cent of Britain's wealth and this is predicted to rise to 60 per cent by 2025.

Similarly, in Australia, 14 of the 200 people in the annual *BRW* Rich List are women. Twelve of the US *Fortune* 500 companies are run by women. High-earning women are spending money, buying things for themselves that may traditionally have been a gift from a male partner.

The growth in women's financial independence and power is shaping industries, communication methods and consumer demands as businesses attempt to remain relevant with this group of decision-makers. It is also having massive implications for general business methods, as women respond extremely well to collaborative business practices.

The female leadership crisis

Despite this, large corporates still fail to have an equal representation of male and female leaders.

It makes economic sense to engage and collaborate commercially with women to gain balanced insight and leadership as part of strategic decision-making for the future. If women are in fact making 80 per cent of household purchasing decisions then they are equally able to add weight to discussions about innovation, new product development, marketing and consumer engagement and customer service strategies. At the end of the day, who better to get inside the mind of a female shopper than women themselves? Forward-thinking companies understand they need women to figure out how to market to women.

As female financial independence and earning power increases, women's spending tends to focus on the people they support versus materialistic purchases. Innovation across industries is required to determine the best way to leverage the growth of female buying power, and innovation by women as leaders is the ideal scenario.

Despite all the positives, women continue to remain the world's greatest underdeveloped and underused source of labour, with nearly one half of working-age women not currently active in the formal global economy. Australia, as a first-world nation, has one of the lowest rates of educated women participating in the workplace despite having one of the highest rates of tertiary education for women.

Research shows us that gender-balanced organisations report increased teamwork and improved consumer insights. The Catalyst report of 2004 entitled 'The Bottom Line: Connecting Corporate Performance and Gender Diversity' illustrated improved corporate performance with a gender-balanced workplace, and almost ten years later a 2013 UK government report, 'The Business Case for Equality and Diversity', found evidence to support gender diversity. This report concludes that businesses actively supporting and engaging a culture of diversity and equality create a positive impact on business performance, risk assessment and decision-making and witness improved company culture and overall increased staff retention. According to the 2013 Male Champions of Change report, 'Tapping into the full talent pool will give us a diversity advantage, creating commercial, societal and economic value'.

According to 'Growing under the radar: an exploration of the achievements of million-dollar women-owned firms', the number of $10 million-plus women-owned firms in the US increased by 57 per cent between 2002 and 2012. Investors are increasingly looking at women-led businesses as places to invest. The Center of Venture Research in the US found that in 2012 nearly 20 per cent of annual investors chose to invest in women-led business.

There is no doubt that unconscious bias continues to challenge the achievement of true equality in society and the workplace. According to the McKinsey and Company report 'Changing

Companies' Minds about Women', invisible barriers continue to exist:

> The last generation of workplace innovations—policies to support women with young children, networks to help women navigate their careers, formal sponsorship programmes to ensure personal development—broke down structural barriers holding women back. The next frontier is rolling invisible barriers: mindsets widely held by managers, men and women alike that are rarely acknowledged but block the way.

Unless we collaborate, the lack of female leaders now will drastically affect the pipeline of female leaders for tomorrow. There will be no funnelling of talent, no mentoring or active sponsoring of younger women — because the senior female leaders simply won't be there to see these things put in place.

The lost investment in talent — in smart, savvy, knowledgeable and strong women who are able to make a difference and ensure that equality is kept — is astonishing, and yet organisations are willing to let this happen and incur the cost to re-recruit versus retain. The reduction in the effectiveness of collaborative business is also clear, with the 'female voice' being lost and key characteristics and strengths disappearing from the process.

The disappearing female leader means a management team devoid of perspective. Decision-making is one-dimensional. To commercially collaborate successfully, to future-proof business, careers and success, we all need to, as Sheryl Sandberg said, 'lean in'.

Improved diversity, and in turn improved collaboration, make sense on so many levels, creating a positive impact on:

- corporate culture
- the cost of employee recruitment
- society and family dynamics

- corporate profitability
- improving business insight and innovation
- the available talent pool.

As Brian Hartzer, Westpac's chief executive officer of Australian financial services, says:

> To me, productivity is really about three things: being more innovative, helping more people get into and stay in the workforce and, most of all, it's about helping people achieve their full potential. What does that have to do with gender equity? Well, everything. We know innovation comes with diversity of thinking. We know diversity in executive teams and in the boardroom helps drive better financial results. We know the rise in female employment has boosted Australia's economy by 22 per cent since 1974. And we know closing the gap between male and female employment rates would boost GDP by up to 13 per cent. That's why it makes economic sense for Australia.

Listen to what the women in society and in business are saying right now. Explore the possibilities of what diversity and 100 per cent involvement could bring—how the benefits of a collaborative society and workplace, one that is well-rounded, well influenced and well distributed, can widen perspective and create opportunities that have not as yet been tapped into. The increasing influence of women is challenging us all to adapt and realign ourselves to the needs of a new society. Engaging women in the workplace, especially at the leadership level, is an essential part of the new collaborative economy.

My generation

We have four generations of people at work together—Baby Boomers, Gen X, Gen Y and Gen Z—often all in the same workplace, each bringing with them a different work ethic, expectation of leaders and companies and belief in their future. Naturally, the different attitudes created by the society in which they were born do not always align—nor are the different generations taught how to work together.

These significant differences of societal expectations are on the one hand exciting in terms of the opportunities they create to share, learn and grow, and on the other are potentially debilitating as instead of seeking to understand and collaborate, many attempt to maintain control, order and stability. 'Old school' Baby Boomer leaders hastily label Gen Y as disloyal and having a poor work ethic; Gen Y label Baby Boomers as uncreative, stuck in their ways, unable to see the opportunity at their fingertips; and Gen X are forever stuck in stasis, not feeling as though they should rock the boat for fear of losing their jobs and security. And yet the opportunity to include the younger generations, those who have been raised to naturally question, to challenge thinking, to consider different options and perspectives, is exactly what we need if we are to future-proof business and careers.

Generation Y (those born between 1977 and 1994) are the largest group of people to enter the workforce since the postwar baby boom. Currently numbering approximately 71 million, Gen Y kids are generally incredibly sophisticated technology-wise, and immune to most traditional forms of marketing and sales as they've seen it all and been exposed to it all since early childhood. According to William J. Schroer, they are less brand loyal, more segmented than previous generations and more involved in family purchase decisions than ever before. They are curious about the future, seek connection, are early adopters of technology and have no fear of simply getting on with it. A generation that is used to taking gap years, travelling the world on a budget, exploring new cultures, engaging with new technologies and actively sharing ideas and thoughts is one that can only add to our thinking.

Today's disrupters and early adopters tend to fall into the Gen Y demographic. With big dreams and no perceived barriers, an increasing number of entrepreneurs under 30 are shaking the traditional infrastructures and strategies of business to create waves of change. These entrepreneurs are leaving an indelible mark on our society. They are savvier, more confident and less risk averse than previous generations. They are the most educated and most technologically skilled generation.

We have witnessed apparent overnight success as Millennials leverage the digital revolution to disrupt industries — Facebook changed the way we connect with friends, Instagram changed the way we share photos, and online games are reaching extraordinary heights in daily revenue takings. These young entrepreneurs are innovating and delivering new products, services and solutions that significantly influence consumer and human behaviour.

An experience in 2010 changed Chase Adam, a member of Gen Y, forever. Chase was serving as a Peace Corps volunteer in Costa Rica. One day he was travelling on a bus through Costa Rica when a woman boarded and asked the passengers for donations to pay for her son's medical treatment. The other passengers on the bus started giving this stranger money, and it was at that moment that the idea for Watsi was born — a non-profit organisation where funds can be raised via crowdsourcing to fund life-changing medical care for people in need. Since August 2012, the company has raised more than $2 million for patients. In an interview, Chase was asked how he built an audience. His response: 'Ourselves. Family. Friends. Friends of friends. Friends of friends of friends. Then strangers'. Now *that's* collaboration in action.

Generation Z (born between 1995 and 2012) will bring with them renewed awareness again, increased knowledge and no doubt new demands on employers — never mind that they'll be applying for roles that don't yet exist. Gen Z will further push society to evolve, placing renewed demand on individuals and organisations to listen, be aware and innovate accordingly.

Yet it is wrong to dismiss Gen X and the Baby Boomers out of hand. They are the current leadership pool, and it is their behaviour that Gen Y and Gen Z will learn and imitate. If they are encouraged to embrace collaborative business methods then it is only to our advantage. It will also assist gender equity in the workplace, as it is the older leadership groupings that are most resistant to change.

The reality is that the demographics of society are changing and organisational structure and working conditions are not keeping pace.

The eternal seesaw

There is constant media coverage and debate on work-life balance. And it's true — now, more than ever, we are struggling with the challenges that modern life presents. But if you look at it through the eyes of the press, it's an issue that is affecting only half of the world's population: women.

And this simply isn't true.

The ongoing images in the media are those of working mums juggling phones and laptops, power dressed with their hair severely pinned up, with bubs on hips and a look of weary resignation on their faces.

The reality is that we *all* want choice. Whether you are male or female, the debate about balance is the same, and the choice to do what you want, when you want is one that affects everyone — whether it be about work, family or whatever you are truly passionate about.

But there are problems that are exclusive to women, and these are the ones that need to be addressed — not the stereotypes of women struggling to 'keep it all together'.

The big issues are that choices for some women are taken away due to the cost and availability of child care, lack of flexible working conditions and, sadly, and incredibly for today, women still earning only 83.5 cents to every dollar male counterparts receive.

The stats still don't stack up in females' favour.

A survey by the Australian Bureau of Statistics in late 2012 of 357 500 working women with a child under two revealed

18.8 per cent faced discrimination in the workplace and 29.3 per cent left the workforce permanently while pregnant or after having their child.

Of those who did return to work, one in four said it was to 'keep their employers happy'.

To save costs, grandparents were the preferred child-minding option for 87900 parents (42.8 per cent) compared to 57700 (28.1 per cent) who used day care.

The research showed that, as a result of their competing responsibilities, 31200 women felt they received negative comments from their manager or colleagues, 22900 said they missed out on a promotion, 10100 reported their duties were changed without consultation, 4500 were demoted and 1200 said their hours were changed without consultation.

These statistics are not just bad news for both women and men who are trying to be change-makers and leaders. They are frightening and disturbing. This is not the way it should be.

Co-parenting is not valued in work terms here as it is in countries such as Sweden, where both parents are entitled to 480 days of parental leave when a child is born or adopted. This leave can be taken by the month, week, day or even by the hour. In terms of equality in the workplace, the positive story continues there: in 2012, the share of women heading companies — private and public sector combined — was 36 per cent compared with 29 per cent in 2006.

More and more couples are making decisions about who will stay home to raise the children based on who has more earning potential versus the traditional gender norm. Men are becoming more visible in new roles. The number of stay-at-home fathers in the UK has risen tenfold in the past decade. There is starting to be some acknowledgement of a more equal weight between the role of mother and father: last year, the US State Department decided to make US passport application forms more 'gender neutral' by removing references to 'mother' and 'father'.

Challenges for work-life balance are only growing, as increasing numbers of families are dispersed around the world. As a result the extended family support network doesn't exist in the same way it used to. There are more and more single parents heading up households and juggling work with raising children. The increased cost of living makes it difficult to survive on one salary. The need to care for aged parents is set to become a major challenge in the next few years.

There is a generational shift underway, with men wanting a greater role in caring for their children. There is more pressure on organisations to evolve workplace policies, making it possible for both parents to manage parenthood in a more balanced fashion.

The work-life balance debate is evolving to become more about choice. It is not gender specific; it is an expectation of a changing society. The division between work and life is becoming defunct as individuals, irrespective of gender or age, make choices that are right for them. What is true is that increasing numbers of people are talking about creating more balanced lives, and this is placing pressure on workplaces and organisations to innovate and evolve how they operate into the future.

~ ~ ~

Evolution in society is driving change and bringing new thinking, insight and solutions to existing problems. Ignore the diversity of opinion at your peril.

Women need to be actively engaged, their input valued; and they themselves must have the courage to step up and step into the collaborative space.

Entrepreneurs need to collaborate to continually evolve, challenge parameters and disrupt the status quo with new products, services and solutions.

Generations need to value each other's strengths and knowledge, respect fully what each brings to the table and appreciate that together we can create waves of change that will secure everyone's future.

And business overall needs to step into the space of commercial collaboration, embracing the opportunity that exists when it builds diverse teams and creates the freedom to discuss, debate and ideate, where the strength of individual thought leadership, skills, expertise and experience can be reinforced through working together.

Business practice changes

New business practices, workplace organisation and external relations are all areas that are being challenged to evolve in response to greater societal forces. Accelerator groups, co-working spaces, flexible working conditions and open-plan working hubs are all being created in response to the need to innovate and evolve as a team and future-proof business. A recent KPMG Australia report, 'Managing Successful Innovation', shared that building a *culture* of innovation is the most critical factor in a company's ability to innovate successfully. The report highlighted the important role of human capital and ensuring the right fit of people to create a team that is open to innovation. Nurturing a culture that lives and breathes innovation is key to future-proofing success. Innovative leaders should recruit people who believe in making the impossible possible.

All of these organisational 'streams' involve one basic principle: that of collaboration. None of them can function without that basic equation of:

Innovation + Decision + Teamwork

For any leader, for any business, this is a very big wake-up call for the future; think team, think nurture, think pioneer.

In terms of driving wealth creation on a global scale, the entrepreneurs (outside corporate) and intrapreneurs (inside corporate) are everywhere creating new businesses, services and products, and many economists believe that entrepreneurship will be the major force behind economic financial stability over the coming years. The spirit of entrepreneurism and innovation is alive and kicking in many countries. In the US, according to the Small Business & Entrepreneurship Council, there are approximately 28 million small businesses. Australia is placed second behind the US in the Global Entrepreneurship Monitor 2011 report. Entrepreneurs' general agility of thought, willingness to adapt, speed to market and pioneering spirit are placing pressure on the traditional business structures, strategies and market delivery.

But even young entrepreneurial businesses will need to continually innovate and evolve their business practices and structures. As they grow, they are fortunate in that they can take the good from the 'old' way of business and adapt it to the new ways that support growth, scale and leveragability while maintaining speed to market, teamwork, agility of thinking and decision-making.

The emphasis on teamwork cannot be strong enough. Responding with agility and decisiveness to the market demands of continuous innovation and invention cannot be done alone. It requires the complementary skills of a group of extraordinary disrupters. The best leaders recognise not only that they do not hold all of the answers but that a team will spark ideas and innovations if everyone is willing to come to the table with their game switched on, knowing that the sharing of thoughts and ideas will create magic.

A collaborative approach is integral, not only in terms of business structure, strategy and vision, but also in terms of culture and policy. Businesses have to be curious and explore the opinions and knowledge within and outside their own organisations. As individuals, and more so as effective leaders, we need to add to our own expertise by actively listening and embracing the ideas of others. We must be constantly curious about the 'what if's'; we have to be prepared to try and fail, evolve and succeed. We need to develop environments for our teams that support innovative thinking and creative problem-solving. We need to adopt the new operating system of commercial collaboration to unlock opportunities to cross-fertilise ideas, skills and knowledge, breaking traditional business boundaries and creating new solutions to existing problems.

Within a team environment, a collaborative space, the smart leader finds that fast-track thinking and decisiveness become easier and easier to deliver. Why? Because by sharing you encourage active discussion, debate and the exchange of ideas. The freedom to discuss facilitates the re-interpretation of ideas, the chance to create something new, to disrupt and discover the unexpected. It engenders trust, which in turn engenders honesty and transparency. Bigger and better solutions are delivered. Change-makers and disrupters are engaged in a possible future.

Cui bono — who benefits — from this approach? It could be:

- *The consumer*, who reaps the benefits of the innovative team thinking and the resulting end product, idea or application.

- *The team*, who are in an environment of growth, safety and collaborative thinking.

- *The business*, which grows exponentially as a result of the increased teamwork and innovative thinking.

- *The leader*, who is able to shift the business forward with a supportive and engaged team delivering the vision.

The opportunity to future-proof is there for the taking. Commercial collaboration must become the backbone of the inventors, innovators and game changers.

Summary

> Rather than being threatened by the volatility of today's climate, the innovative leader will see this as the opportunity for growth and development.

> Opportunity is at the juncture of innovation, socio-economic change and the shift in corporate models.

> Innovation provides an ideal catalyst for change, particularly through driving business growth.

> Smart organisations will not ignore socio-economic changes, as their impact on business will be constant.

> Embracing the changing demographics of the workplace and being curious about the opportunities active and diverse discussion can bring is vital.

> The increasing influence of women cannot be ignored.

> Business structures, policies and cultures have to evolve to future-proof.

chapter 3

Bye-bye beige

The world today is far more connected and fast changing than ever. Leadership and innovation can come from anyone, anywhere, but it's up to the people who lead people in the workplace to create the environment where this can happen. Today and in the future we will need a new mindset of leadership which recognises that the potential of people at work is greater than ever, if they are inspired, supported and aligned with a strong common purpose.

— *Steve Vamos, president, Society for Knowledge Economics*

Beige leaders lead beige companies. Beige companies remain steadfast in the status quo — and a self-propagating disaster begins.

Commercial collaboration is absolutely a choice. It requires us to be open to opportunity and to create freedom for debate and to share ideas. It is about having a willingness to engage with others and the curiosity to listen and learn. It is about being courageous and having challenging conversations with a diverse range of people who are not only cross skilled, but also cross functional and across all demographics.

Commercial collaboration requires a shift from Me to We. The future needs us all as leaders to step up and see the wonderful colour wheel of opportunity that exists when we embrace the potential diversity of opinions, ideas and value systems. It's a well-known fact that trends come and go. For both consumers and business, needs and wants change over time — and in this volatile and increasingly rapidly evolving world, it is difficult to predict and plan for whatever the next latest and greatest thing will be. Companies and leaders need to keep ahead of the curve, listen to customers and act accordingly. They need to constantly evolve and adapt to survive.

Accordingly, to not shift from Me to We is to stay in stasis and to live a life contrary to that potential colour wheel; to live a life of beige. Why? Because one of the biggest things driving business failure is 'beige' leadership. And beige leaders lead beige companies.

Beige leaders are those who are complacent in their role of 'superiority'. They are accepting of traditional methods, and the way things have always been done. They will not entertain change and are closed to new ideas and creative thinking. They often lack vision and foresight, existing in the present and remaining closed to the possibilities of what could be. As a consequence they are unable to inspire others and find it difficult to work effectively within a team environment, particularly with those who are forward looking and curious about the possibilities of the future.

Beige leaders sit comfortably in the squishy status quo sofa, often more concerned with survival than growth. And they have become so ingrained in their comfy corner of the management couch that they forget about the customer. They are often seen by the customer, lower management and personnel as egotistical and arrogant. Empathy, humility, vulnerability and personal disclosure — they see these character traits as signs of weakness, because this is what they were taught.

Beige leaders lead beige companies, and it is a self-propagating disaster heading in one direction: down a slippery slope to failure. Beige companies:

- find it difficult to compete with new players entering the market and challenging their products or services, delivering solutions that are better, quicker and even cheaper in some cases

- are secretive and insular; decisions are made behind closed doors. Mandates are shared in mass format. Meetings consist of 'tells' and the nodding of heads — and the real debate happens in hushed voices at the water filter or coffee machines

- lose customers as, unsurprisingly, they move their allegiance to the new kid on the block who is offering a better product with improved functionality or service and a value add to them, the client

- struggle to attract, recruit and retain talent. They fail to navigate the rapid changes that are happening in the marketplace and the leadership is unable to create a vision for the future. Staff become disengaged, products become stale, business slows down and profits decline

- churn through the day making small adjustments and readjustments in the hope that these small actions will spark significant momentum in a rapidly changing world — but of course it is a mere blip.

The result?

Beige companies fail to stop their own decline, and thus fail to future-proof themselves. Examples of beige leadership and beige businesses are everywhere.

Atari — leader to retrogamer

Atari, once the forerunner of the video game market, has now been relegated to the filing cabinet of nostalgia, a spot for 1980's sitcoms and today's retrogaming trend.

Throughout the 1970s and 1980s, Atari was the pioneer and forerunner of the arcade game, home video game and home computer market. Atari's PONG and the Atari2600 created a multimillion-dollar industry that, during its golden years, delivered sales of more than 30 million consoles and hundreds of millions of games.

So where did it all go wrong?

In the 1980s competition intensified. In 1983 Nintendo launched the Nintendo Family Computer (the Famicom) in the Japanese market and achieved success. Nintendo's plans were much bigger than the domestic market. Their vision was international expansion, and they offered Atari the chance to sells its product in North America under the Atari name. Negotiations commenced, questions were asked, disruption was debated but no agreement could be reached and Atari failed to sign the final contract papers.

In the end, Nintendo decided to go it alone and entered the North American market.

Atari stayed beige while the competition developed and evolved. Supply outgrew demand, the market became saturated and in 1983 the glut of software products resulted in a video game market crash in North America. Atari's financial problems went from bad to worse. Its days were numbered.

Nintendo, meanwhile, saw the crash coming and added a lockout system to its console to stop the use of unlicensed software with its technology and enforce strict licensing standards. It went on to achieve great success, and its iconic Super Mario franchise continues to evolve.

The digital revolution and evolution of smartphones and multi-use platforms continues to challenge the gaming industry, and no doubt further disruption is on the cards. What is certain is that beige leadership will not cut it in this industry. Disruption and change is necessary to secure Nintendo's future unless it wants to join Atari in the retrogaming world. According to CEO Satoru Iwata, 'Given the expansion of smart devices, we are naturally studying how smart devices can be used to grow the game-player business. It's not as simple as enabling Mario to move on a smartphone.'

Blockbuster no more

Blockbuster's demise from its 2004 peak of 9000 stores and a total revenue of $5.9 billion was a result of market changes and a poor leadership response to the changing marketplace. Blockbuster fulfilled a consumer need, enabling consumers to rent movies at a fraction of the purchase price. The model worked in the early days, with consumers happy to be able to find a movie of their choice, rent it and watch it in the comfort of their own home.

In the end, demise was inevitable. The digital revolution, the decline of the movie industry itself and beige leadership within the organisation resulted in a failure to respond to the changing market conditions (and the industry itself), resulting in Blockbuster becoming a convenience store. If video killed the radio star, then downloads killed the DVD-rental store.

The reality is the consumer need never changed—they always wanted value, convenience and access—it was the solution to the problem that changed. The availability of digital downloads and being able to watch movies anytime, anywhere without travelling to a store won the battle in the end. The business model and problem solution, delivery of movies to the end customer, evolved.

And those leaders who questioned the future, Netflix for example, developed perspective and insight into what could happen. They saw an opportunity to disrupt the status quo and they are the ones that ultimately changed the game and survived.

A Kodak moment?

Kodak declared bankruptcy in early 2014. One hundred and ten years before, they had transformed the photographic market with the introduction of the automatic snapshot camera. Capturing a 'Kodak moment' became an everyday turn of phrase as Kodak successfully targeted females in the household and focused its marketing efforts on engaging with soccer mums eager to capture and share their children's sporting efforts. This strategy worked—up to a point.

The invention of the digital camera and associated technologies changed the market forever. Digital cameras became accessible and easy to use, with instant results and 'professional' tools, allowing people to craft, retouch and edit imagery themselves. Kodak watched and took note but failed to respond, choosing not to evolve and instead stick to its existing beliefs about the industry and its tried-and-tested solutions. Kodak chose not to listen to consumers or respond to changes in market conditions. A lack of courage resulted in decisions that maintained the status quo. The Kodak leadership team didn't see the disruption that digital technology would bring to the business, ultimately changing the landscape forever. It was well and truly entrenched in a moment in time. It failed to question the momentum that was starting, becoming disengaged from its customer base, its narrow perspective blinding it to the future obsolescence of its product (the automatic snapshot camera that required film processing and, most of all, delayed gratification).

The beige leadership team was afraid to enter uncharted territory and, instead of upsetting the apple cart, status quo was the strategy of choice.

The absolute bottom line was this: the market had shifted, new distribution channels had opened up and new solutions to customer needs had been developed and launched with commercial success. The new instantaneous nature of photo delivery, the ability to share images in the cloud and craft photographic results in a million ways changed the market forever. There was no going back to the glory days of old. Digital cameras, smartphones and photographic apps would dominate the photographic market. Kodak could no longer compete — and it died from a lack of trying.

Beige won't cut it anymore

Beige leaders more often than not are in survival mode, keeping their heads down, and hoping that by keeping things moving along at a 'steady as they come' pace, their future will be secured. Similarly, beige companies show low levels of active contribution and collaboration, preferring a hierarchical, top-down approach, telling teams what needs to be done rather than consulting with them. Debate isn't entered into, and questioning is seen as negatively challenging leadership decisions, which gives an end result of minimal staff engagement and involvement. Leaders and managers direct; those down the ranks do. This creates a team of plodders who are simply waiting for their next pay cheque or for something better to come along.

According to a Gallup State of the Global Workplace worldwide survey, only 13 per cent of employees are actively engaged at work. To put it another way, approximately 180 million employees in the 142-country study are disengaged — yes, they are going to work and going through the motions of doing their jobs, but they are unlikely to be collaborating and making positive contributions to their employers and organisations. Engagement levels vary across different global regions, with the Gallup report sharing that the US and Canada have the highest level of engaged workers (29 per cent) followed by Australia and New Zealand (24 per cent).

Philosopher Charles Handy talks about the phenomenon of the 'Sigmoid Curve'. According to Handy, the best time to start a new 'curve' is before you reach the peak of your existing one. That way, you will be starting something new when you still have the resources, and the spirit, to take it to new heights. In contrast, most people think of doing something new only when they have reached the bottom of what they are presently involved in.

Successful industries are constantly reinventing themselves. Thus, to remain relevant in tomorrow's world, beige 'leaders', in whatever format, need to be removed and replaced so a new curve can be started. In their place — in the new 'curve' — we will find strength, inspiration and influential leadership from those individuals who are authentic. Leaders who are equally aware of their own unique values and strengths, as well as their weaknesses.

Beige leadership simply won't cut it anymore. Its curve is complete. We need leaders who are so comfortable in the space that they have the strength to lead and share, to learn and grow, to be actively curious and willing to give.

These leaders are capable of amplifying others; they build a culture that encourages and enables sharing, a culture of commercial collaboration that drives change and innovation. These leaders create the space and freedom to think, debate and ideate. This is a culture in which people from diverse skill bases, demographics, genders and industries have the opportunity to speak and be heard.

Beige leadership and the self-propagating disaster that shadows it every day has an ever-shortening life span as innovation, business structure and cultural and societal changes evolve at an increasingly rapid speed around them. This speed of change will expose those beige leaders who hide behind their titles and business cards, and taking their place will be leaders who are able to see around corners, identify opportunities and predict a future that leverages the changing business and consumer landscape. Boston Consulting Group states that organisations must today shift their business model and leadership skills to become more adaptive, to be better, faster and more economical than their competitors. The *Harvard Business Review* supports this sentiment in the article 'The Work of Leadership' by Ronald A. Heifetz and Donald L. Laurie: 'It's tough when markets change and your people within the company don't'.

Leaders of the future

> *Leadership is the challenge to be something more than average.*
>
> — Jim Rohn, author of *The Art of Exceptional Living*

The leaders of the future are the ones that are authentic, see the value in collaborative working and create the space and freedom to ideate regardless of gender, race, age or seniority.

They zig while others zag. They are agile, action-driven and results-oriented. They are focused and directional — strong in commitment and decisive in vision.

We live in a roaringly fast-paced world. The people and businesses that will ultimately succeed will be the ones that are capable of evolution and innovation. They will not only keep their eye on the ultimate goal, but they will be willing to change their dance as required to get there.

The speed of transformation that we are currently witnessing in the way business is being done is challenging us all to think differently. To play on the edge. To seek new opportunity. And above all, to develop innovative ways to communicate our differences, share our authenticity and deliver our products and services.

The leader of the future, the leader in the We space, has to:

- be restless, curious and open to opportunity; evolve and try new things; be looking out for 'what's next' at all times

- combine emotional intelligence with economic intelligence

- balance care for human capital as much as financial capital

- balance quick thinking and decision-making and yet be flexible and open to change

- be agile and keep up with the speed of change

- understand almost perfect is perfect, since the speed of change will make it impossible to get everything right the first time

- have a willingness to not get perfection immediately but to allow perfection to evolve

- collaborate more and be less mindful of hierarchy and position

- be willing to share, mentor others, guide and take a step back

- take an honest and open approach
- create leaders in others and leadership around them
- have a self-belief and inner confidence, an ability to trust themselves and the value they bring to the table.

One thing is certain — beige won't cut it anymore.

Summary

> Beige leadership is a self-propagating disaster waiting to happen.

> Beige leaders will be exposed due to the current speed of change.

> To remain relevant in tomorrow's world, leaders need to become authentic, comfortable in their own space and equally be willing to engage openly with others with a view of constant learning, growth and ideation.

> The leaders of tomorrow are the ones that embrace the value that individuals can bring, are authentic and see the value in collaborative working, and create the space and freedom to ideate regardless of gender, race, age or seniority.

chapter 4

The Me economy

Perhaps adjustment and stabilization, while good because it cuts your pain, is also bad because development towards a higher ideal ceases?

— *Abraham Maslow, psychologist*

The investment in Me as a future-proofing tool is limited unless outwardly engaged in the We economy.

The unprecedented period of change we are currently experiencing, combined with an unknown and uncertain future, is jarring to say the least. With the world evolving at a break-neck speed, and not slowing down any time soon, the digital revolution, globalisation, demographic changes and a hugely increased knowledge base are having a knock-on impact on human behaviour, society's needs and business structures. The uncertainty provided by the global financial crisis (GFC) of 2007–08 has had long-term consequences that continue to play heavily on the minds of our business leaders and individuals as they look to secure profits, sales, jobs and consumers today and into the future.

The solution for many has been to invest in Me; absorbing self-help books, investing in further education, looking to personal growth as a means of self protection and future-proofing — but this self-actualisation is all focused inward. This investment in fact only helps them to help themselves. There is limited outward communication and sharing of knowledge, which in turn limits the creation of further collaborative growth.

Businesses invest in consultants to develop strategic growth plans, human resource strategies, plans to secure tomorrow. Individuals invest in upskilling, reskilling, *more* skilling; they expand their thinking through in-situ workshops and online courses and invest in mentors and coaches to build their self-belief—all in a bid to future-proof their careers.

The volatile, uncertain, complex and ambiguous business world has driven people to find a solution that works for them. Many regress to the relative safety of Me, focusing on their own survival and growth but not necessarily with any active collaboration to help others.

Figure 4.1 shows what happens without collaboration: a complete lack of support for any future-proofing strategies for business or the individuals in them, resulting in stagnation.

The Me industry

Let's get this straight—the starting point is you. You have to believe in yourself, first and foremost. Your dream and vision for yourself and your business future is yours, and until you get this sorted there is no moving forward.

In 1943 Abraham Maslow published his 'Hierarchy of Needs' theory. It presents a pyramid of growth that started with the physiological needs of water, food and sex, moving through to the needs of safety, belonging, esteem and finally self-actualisation. In essence, it states that human motivation is based on people seeking fulfilment and change through personal growth, with self-actualised people achieving all they are capable of. Now that we have food and shelter sorted, survival is about questions of who am I and what is my driver, my 'why?'.

Figure 4.1: what happens without collaboration

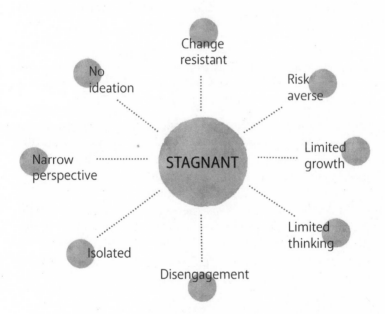

Continuous personal development is an absolute must for those who wish to work within the We space, as long as it is done facing outwards. It's about:

- curiosity and creative thinking
- continually growing and becoming more aware of what you are capable of, the things that are happening around you and the possibilities of what you could leverage
- improving skills and knowledge to become an expert at what you do, on a continuous journey to self-actualisation.

As Jim Rohn said, 'Formal education will make you a living; self education will make you a fortune'.

The need to determine our 'why' has led to a movement of self help, self discovery and growth, of developing self-belief and ensuring you are the best version of yourself, resulting in a whole industry devoted to self-help and wellbeing.

Life coaching has become the second-highest growth industry in the world. According to reports, 40 per cent of Fortune 500 executives in the US and Canada have a coach, and research in Australia indicates that our executives and business leaders are not far behind. The International Coaching Federation (ICF) defines coaching as 'partnering with clients in a thought provoking and creative process that inspires them to maximise their personal and professional potential'. In a 2009 study the Chartered Institute of Personal Development found coaching was used by 90 per cent of the organisations surveyed.

The Me industry is one of high growth:

- According to the 2013 IHRSA Global Report, the global fitness and health club industry generates more than 75 billion US dollars in revenue.
- Spending on anti-ageing products is expected to reach $291.9 billion by 2015, according to a Global Industry Analysts report.
- According to Austrade, the Australian natural (complementary) healthcare industry had domestic sales

of more than $2 billion per year (as at the end of 2011) and predictions are that the popularity of natural healthcare products is growing at a rate of 7 per cent year on year.

In Kathryn Schulz's 2013 *New York Magazine* article, 'The Self in Self-Help', she states that we have 'developed an $11 billion industry dedicated to telling us how to improve our lives'.

Why does this industry exist? Because everyone wants to secure their future in an uncertain world. And when the world is uncertain, the only thing that we can control is ourselves.

The growth of the Me economy has been necessary as people move towards independence, belief in possibility and belief in themselves. And this must continue with every generation. Given the significant growth of the Me economy in recent years, the self-actualisation path is well and truly trodden for many. Constant learning and exploration, goal-setting and values realignment, cementing individual purpose and goals are all necessary, but the self-actualisation is facing in one direction alone — inward.

Evolving from Me to We

The next step of growth is to collaborate. To move from the inward-looking, self-centric Me place to an outward-facing perspective where creative thinking and collaboration exist. Evolving from Me to We is where future-proofing begins as ideation evolves and strategic growth plans are hatched.

The real shift happens when we have the courage and confidence to take all we have learned and look outward. It happens when we:

- move out of the closed-door boardrooms and corner offices and lower the personal barriers that prevent transparency and authenticity

- connect and share our thoughts, ideas and solutions to create better strategies

- actively engage with others, sharing our personal strengths and skills and open up to help, advice and new connections

- enter conversations and meetings with a mindset of curiosity, innovation and invention — an interest in what could be.

When these things happen, we enter the We economy.

Those businesses and people that collaborate diversely, across industries, across sectors and across areas of specialisation are the ones that will create future-proof strategies. They are evolving their thinking; they are developing new solutions, new products and services, new ways to communicate and new technologies.

Matthew Keighran is the managing director of Hugo Boss, Australia. When asked to share his views on the difference between operating in the Me economy and operating in the We economy, his response was as follows:

> A company can only work when its people collaborate internally — share ideas and best practice across departments and subsidiaries. Without all facets of a business moving, sharing, cross-functioning the ultimate goal of success, however that is defined, will not be achieved. A silo or 'Me' culture cannot effectively contribute to a successful business in the mid to long term. The best workplaces are those that are collaborative. A company can only work when it collaborates internally and externally — across like-minded fields and those left of field. Again best practice, best people, best ideas spark creativity and broaden horizons in a person, a department or a manager and can ONLY contribute to motivation and success.

Keighran goes on to share the philosophy of his own company as working to Five C Values, of which collaboration is one. He believes 'the culture that follows these principles — communication, collaboration, customer focused, constant improvement and commitment — will surely achieve its goals not just financially but in improving staff wellbeing and motivation'.

Figure 4.2 illustrates how a business or individual can become an influencer by increasing the levels of commercial collaboration (take) and contribution (give), and by doing so future-proof its business, career and success.

Figure 4.2: commercial collaboration

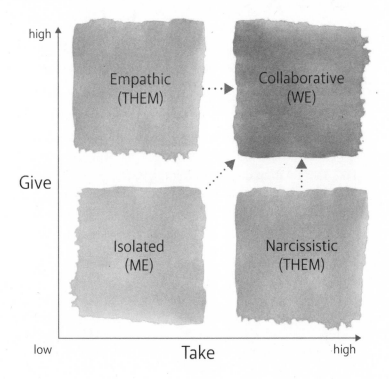

Isolated

Those operating solely in a place of Me are more often than not isolated, in survival mode, keeping their heads down and hoping that by keeping things moving along at a 'steady as they come' pace, their future will be secured.

Narcissistic

Narcissistic leaders and business models are weak on give, yet strong on take. They:

- believe in their own self-worth and importance
- are the takers of business cards and contacts, of knowledge and of ideas and operate heavily in the sell, sell, sell space
- have worked up through the ranks, put in the hard yards and have the resume to prove their self-worth
- believe that they alone have the answers and strategies to drive solutions into the future
- take actively from the group, feeding their business, their ego, their knowledge with low levels of give in return
- do not like to be challenged as leaders and are not open to creating the freedom to openly debate the solution to the problem.

The key word for narcissistic leaders is 'take'.

Empathic

The empathic leader is a willing giver of knowledge, insight, skills and connections — their operating code is one of give, give, give. Giving is their baseline of behaviour and, as such, the empath can often be left depleted of energy, exhausted and feeling as if they constantly give and build others, with no support in return. They want to be everyone's friend, will engage in meetings and invite all to participate. There is a risk that empathic leaders won't make a decision, constantly seeking input and advice from others, concerned about letting people down, upsetting the apple cart. The risk is status quo and failure to disrupt at the fear of upsetting someone within the organisation — let alone the end consumer. The key word here is 'give' — or, to elaborate, giving too much. The empathic leader is constantly giving too much, draining themselves and their organisations of energy.

If a leader is too strong on either side of the spectrum of give or take, creating a shift in business momentum is difficult.

Collaborative

To become collaborative and in the We space, to drive influence and future-proof, there has to be a balance of give and take. The individual or business has to be clear and consistent in:

- what they stand for
- the value and skill that they can share
- the support and help that they require to further thrive.

They can then operate comfortably in a space of commercial collaboration, equally giving to and taking from the group.

Moving from Me to We requires the courage to:

- engage with others
- share expertise for the benefit of the group
- be open and vulnerable
- listen, learn and potentially invest in the ideas and decisions of others.

Increased collaboration and contribution creates influence — one to one, more to more and many to many. It presents an opportunity to disrupt current thinking and enable change-makers to develop strategies, solutions and plans to secure the future.

The most innovative businesses and organisations are starting to develop a system of active collaboration that goes beyond innovation. They have well and truly entered the economy of We, valuing skills from diverse industries and appreciating the value and opportunity the differences create as ideation bubbles to the surface. New products are developed and launched and new solutions to existing problems are implemented with improved ROI — ultimately creating a sustainable future.

To commercially collaborate requires a new operating system: the seven ReConnect Principles to future-proof business, leadership and personal success.

Unlike a drop of water which loses its identity when it joins the ocean, man does not lose his being in the society in which he lives. Man's life is independent. He is born not for the development of the society alone, but for the development of his self.

— B.R. Ambedkar, author of *The Buddha and His Dhamma*

Summary

> Investment in Me is limited unless outwardly engaged in the We economy.

> Operating solely in the Me space is isolating and more about survival than progression.

> The next step is to move from the inward-looking, self-centric Me place to the outward-facing perspective of the We economy.

> The narcissistic leader and business model is weak on give yet strong on take.

> For the empathic leader, give, give, give is their base behaviour, often leading to exhaustion and energy depletion.

> Moving from Me to We requires courage.

> Evolving from Me to We is where future-proofing begins. As ideation evolves, strategic growth plans are hatched and the collaborative leadership style is able to emerge.

Part II

Connections are important. Relationships are important. Trust is important. I call it collaborative innovation — you can have great ideas, but without getting people together who think bigger than you, without participation of the whole group to ensure delivery of a vision — there is nothing. Because it's all about the team. Teamwork. Team thinking. Team participation. That's how you'll have success.

— *Lauren Hall, founder and CEO, iVVY*

chapter 5

Commercial collaboration: the principles

I think victory is hollow when you have no one on your 'team' so to speak to share, excite, inspire and collaborate with. Hollow has no depth, hollow has no energy, and hollow can breed resentment. The 'We' concept invites us to share, to gain traction, to teach more people, to build a bigger and better outcome for all concerned.

— *Shannah Kennedy, author of*
Simplify Structure Succeed

Evolving from Me to We, adopting a new operating system and embracing the opportunity and potential that are created when commercial collaboration is the standard means of operation will future-proof business, careers and success.

So how do you do it? How do you move from Me to We? Shannah Kennedy's quote is an exceptional demonstration of what is positive about the concepts of the 'We' way of thinking. To share, to teach, to build; these are all words that have positive associations. On the 'Me' side there is no energy, no life, no progress: all features of a hollow, inward-looking business model.

The future is volatile. This is not a maybe, but a certainty — perhaps the only certainty there is. Change is therefore critical. In turn, collaboration is the key to change; further, commercial collaboration is critical to future-proofing businesses, careers and personal success as it allows individuals to:

- think differently
- develop a new perspective
- disrupt the status quo
- enable themselves and their businesses to compete long term.

The current juncture of innovation, socio-economic shifts and changing business practices and approaches is creating self-perpetuating momentum for change, and keeping up with change is not something that we can easily do alone. It is a necessity to create customer-centric strategies and evolve business structures and cultures; most importantly, we need *leaders* who are capable of making appropriate decisions when the future is uncertain. Leaders and businesses that are able to do the following will thrive and survive:

- create the necessary freedom to collaborate
- think critically and creatively
- invent and innovate
- understand the importance of collaboration for a better future

Those unwilling to work collaboratively, who prefer to work alone, who are closed to outside thinking and different approaches will slowly disappear.

> *Collaboration is needed in every single great event for mankind. From impressionism to silicon valley, from mapping the genome to trekking Everest ... it has all been collaboration sometimes working in sync and sometimes in competition.*
>
> — Kath Creel, marketing director, Impact AV

To break it down to its simplest points, the future is brightest if we understand that:

- collaboration is key; commercial collaboration is critical to future-proof businesses, leaders and personal success
- the juncture of innovation, socio-economic shifts and changing business practices and approaches is critical to creating:
  - a customer-centric strategy
  - the freedom to think critically and creatively
  - the freedom to invent and innovate
  - the evolution of business culture.

So the critical questions are:

- What do we need to do?
- How do we collaborate commercially?
- How do we future-proof our careers and businesses in the uncertain future?

The model 'Commercial collaboration: The principles' unpacks the nine essential steps that will enable you to answer, 'What do we need to do?'

The seven ReConnect Principles that are covered in chapters 6 to 12 answer the question: 'How do we move from Me to We — to commercially collaborate, to future-proof ourselves, our careers and our businesses?'

Commercial collaboration: the principles

Figure 5.1 (overleaf) illustrates the nine steps of the commercial collaboration principles in the journey from Me to We. At each step there are choices: move forwards or backwards, shift towards the effective collaboration space of We or move back towards the limitations of Me.

Figure 5.1: commercial collaboration—the principles

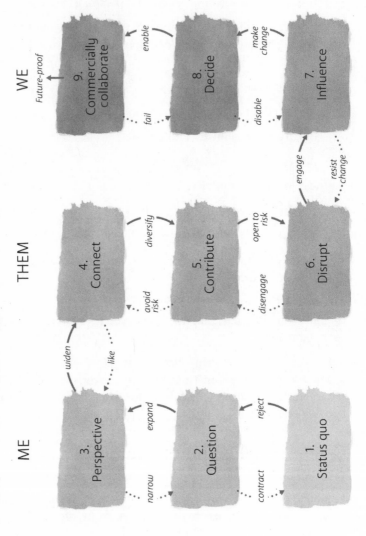

There are three distinct focus levels within this model: Me, Them and We.

- Me is all about taking ownership of Me and the shift required from accepting the status quo to leading in the We space.

- Them is about starting a connection with others and understanding the role of Me within the context of a wider community of connections.

- We is when Me is totally aligned and congruent with the value they have to bring to the group; they have the courage and confidence to give and take and they engage 100 per cent in collaborative working practices that develop innovative thinking.

The 'Me' focus

The first focus level is 'Me'. This has to be the single-minded starting point in the nine-step model to effective commercial collaboration.

It starts with you taking ownership and responsibility for direction, future vision and goals. Despite all the opportunity that collaboration, partnerships and mutual work can create, to make it work commercially and to mutual benefit comes down to one thing: you. If you aren't tough enough or savvy enough, or you don't have enough chutzpah, smarts and business acumen to see the lay of the land, then all the collaboration in the world is not enough to make you or your business succeed.

The Me focus is about taking responsibility for ourselves and understanding the necessity to cultivate and own a skill set or area of expertise, and to have self-belief and inner confidence. To believe that anything and everything is possible. Sometimes what is needed is a collaboration with yourself; a collaboration with Me. The Me focus level requires inward thinking and introspection. It requires analysis of the current situation and opening our eyes, ears and minds to opportunity.

Step 1—Status quo
Understand the current state of play and decide if this is where you and/or your business want to be.

What does status quo actually mean? By definition, it is the 'existing state of affairs'. It means keeping things as they are. In work terms, it means acceptance, even if you aren't necessarily overjoyed by a situation, because you don't want to rock the boat. It means doing things in the same way as always — same procedures, same methods. The result? No change, no initiative, no evolution. The acceptance of the status quo doesn't equate to progress.

The real key, at this stage, is the choice that we make. The choice to accept the status quo or reject the status quo and create a change in activity or behaviour, deciding what we want to be the version of ourselves or our businesses that makes each of us unique and different.

Accepting the status quo results in stagnation. Rejecting the status quo and deciding to change things is the first step in the process.

This is where we see:

- individuals thinking about career and life changes
- businesses considering new markets
- product development teams investing in research and development to find the next big thing
- market researchers identifying gaps
- future thinkers predicting major market shifts.

Step 2—Question
Critical questions develop new insight and highlight new opportunities and solutions. Once status quo is rejected and it is decided that change has to happen, step 2 involves curiosity and asking critical questions such as:

- What change needs to happen and how?
- What does 'next' look like?

- What other skills are needed?
- How can things be improved?
- Where is average being accepted?
- What is stopping further achievement?

Questioning is about gaining new insight. It is about seeking to understand and to explore the possibility of what other options there are. Active questioning increases the knowledge base and enables decision-making.

It is usually at this stage that the individual chooses to invest in self — further education, wellbeing, me time, searching for the next job opportunity. A business will carry out a SWOT (strength, weaknesses, opportunities, threats) and impact analysis, it will review current structures, policies and products, engage researchers and consultants and it will audit capacity and capability against resources.

Throughout this step there is always the chance of regressing to the status quo — it's all too hard, it can't be done, it's out of my control. The questioning contracts and stops as individuals, leaders and businesses decide to accept the way it is versus embracing change.

On the flip side, those who are curious and want to future-proof continue to expand their questioning and naturally evolve to step 3.

Step 3 — Perspective

Perspective brings with it a wider awareness of what action needs to be taken to future-proof. Questioning naturally develops a new perspective, an evolved vision of what could be, a new level of awareness of changes that need to happen to future-proof individuals and businesses. A wide lens at this stage identifies possibilities — of new thinking, products, distribution channels, skills required and resources that need to be sourced. Perspective creates curiosity. It allows you to take what you know, your expertise and unique positioning, and explore how it can be further leveraged and scaled in the wider world. This curiosity opens the door to opportunity.

The three steps of status quo, questioning and perspective form the first focus level of Me. The next step in the commercial collaboration model is seeking out others ('Them') to further evolve thinking, ideation and disruption.

The 'Them' focus

The second focus level is 'Them'. This is the next step towards effective commercial collaboration, where the evolved Me begins to explore the world outside the comfort zone, seeking like-minded groups, researching a wider marketplace and beginning the process of collaboration.

Moving to this level of focusing on Them requires confidence and courage to engage with diverse networks. It involves full disclosure to enable effective contribution and the opportunity that is created when there is an openness and willingness to disrupt.

Step 4—Connect

Building a diverse and powerful network opens doors, pushes boundaries and stretches thinking. Building powerful connections is absolutely necessary for successful collaboration. The shared ideas, contacts, thought leadership, expertise and learnings, if openly discussed, ultimately evolve existing thought processes.

A powerful and diverse network can become your lifeline. Ultimately it is the relationships that you build, nurture and manage that provide a support system to fall back on as required. Equally, the relationships challenge your thinking and decision-making.

As with each of the steps in this model, there is a choice. At step 4, the norm is for people and businesses to connect with like-minded groups of people. Accountants connect with accountants, CEOs connect with other CEOs, small businesses engage with other small businesses. In business, internal meetings traditionally stay within management levels. Directors' meetings are exclusively for directors; marketing planning meetings are only for the marketeers, product planning sits within the creative team. This is okay — to a point. Yes, it provides support and understanding of the conversation parameters and an awareness of the immediate issues at hand. Yes, it provides a safety net, support, idea sharing and connection. And yes, more often than not it drives new thinking and new ideas.

But to push it further and drive true commercial collaboration, connections and groups require diversity of:

- expertise
- status
- gender
- age
- knowledge
- experience
- skill sets
- industry and business function.

Powerful and diverse networks are those that connect cross-functionally, cross-industry and cross–skill base. Diverse connections:

- challenge thinking
- ask questions
- push boundaries
- increase awareness
- open our eyes to another way
- bring to the fore opportunities that were previously not in the direct line of vision
- present solutions that were not previously considered
- create innovations that were once not thought possible.

Step 5—Contribute

A willingness to share skills, expertise and knowledge drives positive change and will build a future business world that is not only smarter but also more rewarding for all.

Contribution only happens when there is willingness to openly share knowledge, insight and expertise. Contribution is not simply about sharing a business card and swapping LinkedIn addresses; it's about engaging in a space of:

- What can I do for you?

- How can what I know or who I know help you achieve your goals?

- How can what I know add value to you and/or your challenge?

The shift towards commercial collaboration happens when those who are connecting are risk tolerant as opposed to risk averse. Risk tolerance in this context requires:

- being open to challenge, debate, new ideas and new thinking

- being willing to zig and zag towards the ultimate goal, to change current thinking, to start again, to try something totally new

- individuals and businesses to be open and honest with vulnerability, fears and weaknesses.

In this step we see:

- businesses presenting to angel investors and venture capitalists

- CEOs engaging with Gen Ys on ideation blue sky meetings

- non-competing yet synergistic businesses sharing intelligence

- PR, promotion, advertising and creative agencies working together to develop integrated solutions to client briefs

- senior executives engaging with junior staff, contributing actively to career growth plans.

Those who are risk averse at this step are afraid to share thoughts and opinions, expertise, knowledge, what's worked and even what's not worked. The risk-averse protect themselves, afraid to share what they know — often out of fear. Those who are risk tolerant, meanwhile, are open to sharing knowledge and being challenged on their own thinking and strategies.

Step 6 — Disrupt

Disruption kick-starts a shift and drives innovation. As diverse connections strengthen and participants value the contributions being made, the space for disruption is created. Ideas start to form, new solutions to existing problems are debated and conversations give birth to new opportunities.

Disruption happens because a need to change has been identified. Disruption creates:

- a shift in behaviour
- the opportunity to change the game
- the chance to create something new.

Disruption is change itself; it is invention, innovation and creation.

Disruption creates new industries (mobile technology), new services (Airbnb), new products (Google glass), new technologies (iBeacons). Disruption creates new alliances and partnerships, new joint visions and dreams.

Again there is a choice to move forwards or backwards. The choice at this step is to engage in the opportunity or to disengage and move back to the safety zone of the known.

~   ~   ~

In the Them level, the three steps of connection, contribution and disruption challenge the Me to stand in the spotlight and use its voice, to have the courage to share knowledge, openly divulge and be willing to learn.

It is during this Them phase that, for some, self-doubt kicks in, belief dissipates and fear takes over. The result? A move backwards to Me and the investment in self. If this self-doubt can be overcome, the individual or business is able to shift into the We space. Confidence and self-belief in expertise and vision enable the active reciprocity, the give and take, to begin.

The 'We' focus

The third and final focus level towards commercial collaboration is the 'We' phase. This is where the investment in Me and Them comes together to create incredible opportunity. It is a place where there is:

- an equal exchange of give and take
- the chance to play and influence at the edge of the comfort zone
- the opportunity to make decisions that will future-proof careers and businesses
- collective intelligence
- the ultimate space of collaboration.

It is during this phase that individuals and businesses truly move from Me to We. It is here that to collaborate is to lead and create the freedom to explore, develop plans and think creatively. To lead is to inspire. Inspiration drives innovation, invention and game-changing strategies that are scalable and leveragable. The We space is one of future-proofing.

Step 7—Influence

Influence is the ability to create action. Influence can change the game. Influence:

- affects behaviour
- alters a course of action or inspires a change in direction
- creates movement and a shift in energy.

In the commercial collaboration model, the influence step is critical. Influence is where individuals, groups and businesses become known for something; we start seeing the game changers, the ones that shake things up, the ones that are focused on their big-picture dream.

Influence requires:

- perspective
- connection
- trust
- authority
- active contribution and disruption, creating a reason for others to care.

Influence cannot be a solo enterprise — it can only exist in the 'We' space. It requires others to:

- support
- lead
- buy in
- follow
- create the momentum
- drive the change.

In this step, individuals or businesses can be resistant to the change that is being presented and resist the influence, moving back into the Them phase, or they can be open to influence, taking on board the contributions and disruption that are being presented. They become part of the evolution. They are the change-makers.

Step 8—Decide

This is where you synthesise information and make a decision to do something different. In step 8 the choice is one of enabling or disabling decision-making. To move to step 9, a place of commercial collaboration, there needs to be a bias towards action, a willingness to make a decision. Making sound decisions is a skill set, and by enabling decision-making, you can quickly make the best choice possible with the information at hand: the information gained from the collective.

Part of this step is understanding that some decisions are good decisions and others fail. Yet it is during the moments of failure that learning happens, evolution continues and the change boundary is pushed further.

On the other end of the choice spectrum, disabling decision-making creates a stop in the energy flow of the collective. The disruption that was discussed and debated, the change creation, is halted in its take-off and remains stuck on the runway.

Step 9—Commercial collaboration

Collaborating with mutual commercial benefit is the new operating system, the key that unlocks a bright future. The final step in the model is the choice between future-proofing or failing. This is a space where:

- energy is expended where it will have the most effect
- collectively and collaboratively, active contribution, disruption, influence and decision-making happen
- the collective energy drives momentum and movement
- if we invest our time and energy, if we are brave, if we are authentic in who we are, we will have the highest return and payoff—and enjoy doing it.

The mutual result and shared success is the glory.

~　~　~

Now that we know the steps, the next challenge is how to carry them out. This is where the seven ReConnect Principles are key. By adopting these principles and embracing the new operating system of commercial collaboration—choosing to move from Me to We—business, careers goals and success goals will be future-proofed.

The seven ReConnect Principles

Chapters 6 to 12 answer the question, 'How do we move from Me to We to commercially collaborate to future-proof ourselves, our careers and our businesses?' Through breaking development — or redevelopment, for many — down to seven basic principles, leaders are taught how to reconnect as:

- team members
- entrepreneurs
- corporate executives
- leaders.

This is not reinventing the wheel. It is based in common sense and an understanding that people of worth and integrity want to evolve and face the volatility head on — with others, with their teams.

Alexx Stuart, creator of the 'Real Food, Low Tox Living' blog, founded her business on a passion and then discovered a community of like-minded people who wanted to collaborate on driving change. Alexx started blogging about Real Food and, within 18 months, without any advertising, built an almost 15000-strong following of people that support her passion and commitment to education, awareness and change. Through her blog Alexx now writes, trains and speaks. She is an active supporter of Jamie Oliver's Food Revolution and her book, *Real Treats*, became a number-one bestseller within 12 hours of its launch. As she says:

> Collaboration amplifies action and change. No thought leader ever changed things on their own. Each one of them used their vision as a starting point for building collaborative movements. The initial ideas can be exciting, but when they're brought to life through collaboration, that's where the magic happens.

The new operating system of commercial collaboration is the seven ReConnect Principles:

1 Be brave

2 Build a diverse network

3 Full disclosure

4 Disrupt

5 Exchange value

6 Think bigger

7 Sponsor others

Case study—learning to collaborate, moving from Me to We

Melissa Browne is the owner of A+TA. She is a tax expert and has a fascination for business management, strategy and why certain businesses are more successful than others. She is passionate about showing business owners how understanding their numbers will help them become more successful, more profitable and less stressed.

Melissa, author of *More Money for Shoes*, is a firm believer in the power of commercial collaboration. Here she details her personal experiences in moving from the Me space to the We space:

> Let me start by saying I loathe asking for help. This might seem like a strange statement in a book about collaboration, however it's the truth. If I'm completely honest, I believe asking for help is a sign of weakness.

> Of course, if someone else was to suggest this I'd tell them they were mad—asking for help is not only sensible, it should be encouraged. Particularly when it comes to business. That's why over my years in business I've tried to step into arenas, tribes and coaching environments

where collaboration is not simply spoken about but actively encouraged. Instead of wearing my unwillingness to ask for help as a badge of honour I have spent many years learning to collaborate.

I say learning to collaborate because asking for help and receiving help does not come naturally to me, as I'm sure it doesn't come naturally to many business owners. However I know that if I rely only on my own resources, I will always be limited. That's because, despite my best wishes, I'm not the best at everything. Of course, I'm very willing to help other business owners—but if I'm not willing to receive in return it's not really collaboration, it's charity, and it doesn't allow the other business owner to grow from giving in return.

I experienced the power of collaboration with my first business, Accounting and Taxation Advantage (A+TA), most powerfully through group coaching with other accounting firms. Instead of being fearful that our ideas might be ripped off or stolen, each firm met each quarter to share what we were doing, share IP, share numbers and how we were performing or underperforming and share ideas that might improve each other's firms. It took some courage to do this I must confess, but the improvements in my business as a result of both the transparency and the drive to improve and chase the bigger firms took my business to a new level.

I learned in this environment that where there is transparency and trust, collaboration can be an incredibly powerful tool as you learn from each other's wins and losses. I now actively seek this through other regular forums, most currently with Entrepreneurs Organisation (EO).

Of course, in order to collaborate I believe that trust and confidence are essentials. Often these can come from belonging to a tribe of other like-minded people. When I was setting up my second A+TA office in North Sydney and launching my book, *More Money for Shoes*, I sought out tribes that had a similar mindset to me. Tribes that actively sought success in business and weren't afraid to chase it.

Initially I thought that doing so might simply help grow my business, however I have discovered the right tribe brings so much more than simply growth. The right tribe allows you to be transparent, vulnerable even, and in that place courage can be found to ask, receive and give help without even realising you are doing so.

I am thankful to have discovered this tribe in the Little Black Dress Group. Around a dinner table, over coffee, via email or at a retreat problems are shared, answers are sought and introductions are made. There is very little fanfare or fuss made. Instead business is exchanged and collaboration simply happens.

Hopefully, it is with my newest venture, Thinkers.inq, that I have finally learned from the arrogance that comes from wanting to do everything myself. With this new venture I have consciously chosen to collaborate with other amazing business owners right from the start. Part of this decision has to do with the large vision my co-directors and I have for Thinkers.inq. Thinkers.inq is long-day early learning centres, and we want to come in and shake up the industry. My co-directors and I believe we will change the way preschool is done in Australia. Of course, with a vision this big, it would be foolish to think we can do everything ourselves. That's why, very early on, we went to our tribes to consciously collaborate with the best people we knew that could help us see our vision through.

We tapped into our networks for the best in market activation, marketing, nutrition and the real food movement, copywriters, photographers and more. We tapped into our social and professional networks for graphic designers and our first crop of amazing teachers. We'll be tapping into all our tribes and more when it comes to marketing, pushing out our message, seeking families, speakers for conferences and sourcing new locations. That's because these people, in these tribes, are the best at what they do. As Richard Branson famously said, 'It's all about finding and hiring people smarter than you'. Often when you're starting out in business you simply don't have the funds to go out and employ either part-time or full-time staff—and, more and more often, it doesn't make sense to. However, collaborating with the best business owners in their field for a win-win for everyone involved does make a whole lot of sense.

I still loathe asking for help. I'll still be tempted every so often to want to do everything myself. However what I know through running both A+TA and Thinkers.inq is that this is an incredibly limiting mindset that will always impede the growth of my business. Instead, being open to how I can help other business owners and how they might be able to help my businesses has created amazing opportunities for everyone to grow and succeed.

Surely that's what business and true collaboration is all about.

chapter 6

ReConnect Principle 1— Be brave

> To operate based on conviction and belief requires an acceptance that your actions could get you fired. This is different from pig-headed bravado, and it is different from putting the company at risk.
>
> — *Simon Sinek, author of* Start with Why *and* Leaders Eat Last

Commercial collaboration requires us to be brave, to step up and have the courageous conversations that drive change.

Instinct in the workplace is a funny thing. Some people are naturally able to give 100 per cent all the time, irrespective of their position within a company, and irrespective of the company they are working for. They have an intrinsic ability to put the best of themselves forward — sometimes knowing full well that this will not necessarily be rewarded in the short term. What it does show, though, to their subordinates, colleagues and those who are perhaps skimming the surface of 'successful' leadership, is the difference between bravery in business and bravado.

It is worrying how many people only show the tip of the business performance iceberg on a continual basis. Many are not willing to expose the majority of their ability, even once firmly established in a role or company, instead choosing to hide it under a slick, smooth surface.

There exists a culture of business bravado. It is the game of bluster and pretence, and false promises. It is the mindset of 'I will give enough to look as though I am performing above expectations while secretly cruising my way to tomorrow, or next week — or my next role'. Business bravado is being content to sit on one's hands while nodding furiously and giving every indication of leading change. It is 'fake it till you make it', not engaging wholly or giving completely — despite having the ability to do so. The sad part is that often more effort is expended on being the equivalent of a business iceberg than giving one's all.

The 'bravado' style of business can be employed by entire corporations. It's often seen in big corporate mergers — less so now than pre-GFC, admittedly, simply because it seems less palatable. However, in May 2014, veteran French industrialist Patrick Kron was faced with accusations of 'secrecy and silence' after failing to notify the government of his plan to sell his company, Alstom, to General Electric. During a debate in parliament Minister of Industrial Renewal Arnaud Montebourg called it a breach of national ethics. Mr Kron accepted the $13.5 billion bid from the US behemoth for his previously state-bailed-out company regardless of government criticism, saying his motivation was never to repeat the disasters of 2003, and that his responsibilities were to Alstom.

But were they? Could his actions be seen as brave, or purely an act of bravado, given the consideration shown him by the French government in the past? Had he shown selfish leadership without considering the wider ramifications of his actions?

In 2012, the ego truly had landed when Japan's Softbank Corp bought out the American telco Sprint Nextel Corporation, with the chief executive, Masayoshi Son, explaining the deal to shareholders and the public in three words: 'I'm a man'.

Because Sprint wasn't a domestic competitor with domestic networks, the deal didn't have any of the typical benefits of telco mergers (redundant networks, overlapping staff). It also left stockholders eventually owning only 70 per cent of the overall corporation, with the rest publicly traded. Masayoshi Son gave no other explanation for the buyout, merely pledging to spend more time in the US at Sprint HQ, and to develop technology that, in fact, the US had already been developing for quite some time. His response to queries about developing existing technology?

'Trust me.'

These examples are on a huge scale, but this attitude translates down to the smallest action. It can be a matter of constantly not speaking up, or refusing to take an active role in the professional development of those coming through the ranks. It can be refusing to disclose one's own actions out of sheer ego. It can be acting 'for the good of the company' by staying quiet when the status quo is not ethically correct.

It all starts with Me. Unless you are comfortable in your own skin and able to stand steadfast, with confidence, in your own spotlight — self-actualise — the shift to We and commercial collaboration cannot begin. See table 6.1 for a comparison of brave leaders, and leaders with bravado.

Table 6.1: bravery vs bravado

A brave leader...	A leader with bravado...
Leads change	Makes excuses
Takes control	Takes beta position
Exceeds targets	Meets targets
Actively mentors others	Invests in self
Undertakes outside learning	Is 'too busy' for knowledge
Takes a collaborative approach	Faces inwards
Is willing to listen	Only hears their own voice
Is open and transparent	Is closed and secretive

Lead

> *Why fit in when you were born to stand out?*
>
> — Dr Seuss, author

If that is how bravado looks, then what is bravery? Bravery is:

- stepping not necessarily always outside the square, but along the edges of the business square
- getting out of the shallowness of surface leadership
- questioning your own position
- taking on leadership
- constantly learning
- posing new sets of challenges for oneself in terms of professional standards and goals.

Bravery is striving to be a change-maker and to improve the way things are done within the company, the sector, the industry, or perhaps even within a community. Bravery is about being courageous in everything you do. It's about having the courage to do the following:

- stand in your own spotlight
- use your voice
- ask for help
- be vulnerable
- be different
- challenge the status quo — because it is through this that change happens.

Bravery is about leaning in. Sheryl Sandberg started the catch cry for women to 'lean in', but this could be a cry for everybody. Be brave, embrace diversity, align yourself with the new operating system of commercial collaboration and lean in to drive change.

Bravery is reaching out to fellow leaders and those who are willing to shape policy and procedure, and giving 100 per cent to drive business forward in an ethical and productive way.

For corporates in particular it is about coming back to the authentic, and to the transparent. It is in many ways taking the lead from entrepreneurial models, where 'bravery' is key to driving sales. The ability to lead by example is also absolutely critical to success in a market that is cynical and sick of inflated salaries — and inflated egos.

In a nutshell, those who through fear or simple laziness are not willing to give 100 per cent of their business selves need to re-think their position.

Taking risks

Jim Donald, the former CEO of Starbucks, and now CEO of Extended Stay America, is an amazing example of someone leading with bravery.

Extended Stay America is a national hotel chain which in early 2013 was just coming back from the brink of bankruptcy. Staff were afraid to risk their jobs by making decisions and disrupting the status quo in any way — even at the eventual cost of the business. Whether it was being afraid to give an unhappy guest a free night's accommodation or make decisions about a property, they were simply too nervous to show any of their own bravery — in other words, they were giving just one-eighth of the business iceberg.

So Jim Donald gave every staff member a safety net. He created miniature 'Get out of jail free' cards, and gave one to each of his 9000 employees. In return for making a risk on behalf of the company, all they had to do was hand them in — no questions asked. Gradually, the cards are being used. One manager in New Jersey cold-called a movie-production company when she heard it would be filming in the area. The film crew ended up booking $250 000 in accommodation at the hotel.

This is a risk, but it's a calculated one. The company had already been in the worst possible position, and the employees were stagnating. Bravery in decision-making was called for, and it got results. Jim Donald acted with honesty, acknowledging that failure is a part of progress, and collaborated with his staff to find a way forward.

Leadership and the ability to influence and make a difference in your own world, your own backyard, is in each and every one of us.

Start with yourself

ReConnect Principle 1 is all about Me and stepping into the space of being brave. If we start with ourselves, managing our own lives and self-belief, then we can each create a difference at the grass roots — this is where we can all make a difference. This is the key message in terms of leading with bravery — it is the need for each of us to take responsibility for ourselves. To understand and appreciate the necessity to cultivate the skill set that is unique to each of us, to have self-belief and inner confidence and to take responsibility for ourselves. To believe that anything and everything is possible.

Without a doubt, there are certain qualities and attributes that some have more than others. But the real key is that we each have a choice as to the version of ourselves we want to be, that makes each of us the unique leader we are.

The only judgement that matters is the one we have of ourselves. If we don't start leading from within, taking control to acknowledge our own values and belief systems and acknowledging the person that we are on the inside, we will never be capable of being the better person on the outside. How can we give to others what we don't have ourselves? How can we teach, guide, mentor and lead others if we haven't set ourselves up for success?

What we know from reading stories of amazing entrepreneurs, CEOs and thought leaders is that the one thing that separates them from the masses — the tipping point that takes them from zero to 100 miles per hour in five seconds flat — is the ability and willingness to have courageous conversations.

Take a look around at those who have changed the game. They have the courage to:

- zig while others zag
- ask the difficult questions — of both others and themselves — to gain a new perspective
- take action with a new perspective
- think differently
- do differently
- be a game changer.

Being a change-maker is risky business. It takes bravery. It takes a level of courage to challenge the traditional or the 'it's always been like that'. It takes an inner confidence and belief to be a non-conformist, to have a viewpoint contradictory to the expected.

Make a difference today to influence the lives of others around you. As John C. Maxwell shared, 'If you are bigger on the inside than you are on the outside, then over time you will become bigger on the outside'.

Amber Daines, CEO of Bespoke Communications, knows exactly what it is like to be in the atmosphere of the Me culture rather than We. She has worked within the very male-dominated print media industry at an international level, which is notorious for secrecy, paranoia and distrust. There was no effort to be open and transparent, from the editorial leaders down to the cadet staff.

She worked her way through the ranks and saw this behaviour repeat itself in the newspaper industry and in PR and the government sector. Finally she made the bravest decision of her working life: to start her own PR agency, Bespoke Communications. Here, her bravery would occasionally get her into hot water — but she also found that it strengthened her collaborative ties with her clients, both external and internal. In Amber's words:

> The exponential value of true collaboration is unquestionable in the super-interconnected business world of today—whether you work with, or within, small business, corporate, government or not for profit. True collaboration only works when there is a mutual understanding of looking after the other individual as much as, or even more than, what you are getting back from any projects, contracts or referrals for new business opportunities. It takes a sense of elevated self-worth to reach out and be able to elevate someone else's prospects even if yours desperately need a lift, but it's also an amazing show of powerful leadership.
>
> Global businesses can no longer be insular, secretive and unaccountable. The people who run them have to be willing to work with others, to learn and teach in equal measure. As the saying goes, 'If you are the smartest person in the room, you are in the wrong room'. Two decades into my career, I have come to agree. The bravest leaders that I admire most listen to their most junior staff as well as their successful elders and can embrace the best ideas of those they may deem their equals or even competitors. Collaboration is what will make the future business world a braver, smarter, and more rewarding place.

Step out of your comfort zone

What does being in a comfort zone mean to you? Does it mean that you are stable and able to cope with day-to-day life without feeling overwhelmed? Maybe — but what it also means is a lack of ability, or perhaps a lack of opportunity, to evolve. It means staying static, not changing, not growing. There is no room for growth, adventure, curiosity, or testing possibilities when you are well and truly stuck in the safety of the comfort zone.

It's easy to get trapped in your comfort zone, and this place becomes the status quo. The place of stagnation. But if you step outside the comfort zone, take a journey to the edge to test the possibilities, it strengthens the Me and gives a massive boost to your self-confidence and self-belief. It empowers and engages. Stepping out of your comfort zone creates a new perspective and with this comes other options and pathways to take. Stepping out of your comfort zone is a brave thing to do.

Imagine if the late Steve Jobs hadn't gone back to Apple as its CEO. If he hadn't invested in Pixar. If he had been happy to say, 'Well, I tried — and it didn't work, so I'll just stay where I'll be comfortable'.

No iMac. No iPhone. No iPad. No visionary steering Apple to extraordinary heights.

Think of Instagram launching despite a declining market and against all advice. As Facebook founder Mark Zuckerberg said, Instagram was a company with 'lots of buzz but no business model' — but it didn't stop him from buying it for US$1 billion in September 2012. He recognised the potential of what its creators had seen from the start. And they only saw it because they were prepared to take a chance. They stepped a long way out of their comfort zone — or should that be #comfortzone?

There is no denying that stepping out of the safety of where you are most comfortable is scary as hell. It often means big ups and downs — a rollercoaster rather than a gentle turn on the merry-go-round. You will probably feel as though you are without a safety net much of the time, and that can be extremely confronting.

But just imagine the possibilities.

In business, and in life, there is no free ride. However, we get fantastic opportunities if we are lucky, and often we are too 'comfy' to recognise them for what they are. It is those people who are willing to challenge themselves, who make themselves accountable for their own success, and ultimately their own happiness — who recognise that the need to reach that little bit further or higher — who end up with the biggest satisfaction. It is those who take the leap who are able to collaborate with others to mutual commercial benefit with confidence.

Own your unique value system

Being brave means understanding what makes up your value system and owning it. Living it and working it. This system is unique to you and it's your responsibility to take ownership. There are times when it will be challenged or when you will give in to others' values — and you will look back and kick yourself, and wish you had trusted your intuition. That intuition, that gut feeling? Don't ever mistrust it. It is a key part of you, and you should learn that it is one of your best assets. Ignore it at your peril.

Organisational culture is not created — it is the culmination of behaviours and value systems. Organisational culture cannot be created through workshops, consultant input, a printed and framed statement on the reception wall or in the CEO's office. It is something that develops as a result of the vision, behaviours, actions and values of the entire team, driven fundamentally from the top.

Consistency of action and walking the walk of value systems and behaviours builds an organisational culture over time that is understood by all, trusted by all and believed by all.

This is why, as business leaders, it is imperative that we are individually clear on our value systems, that we live and breathe these values in every behaviour, decision and action we take, trusting our own unique leadership style to achieve the best for our own success, our team's success and the financial success of the company.

If we are to create the organisations that we want to work within that we want others to enjoy being part of, and to build a company that is more than just the service or product that is being sold, the soul of the organisation has to permeate everything … and it's more than just words.

Start talking the talk and walking the walk every day.

Stand in your spotlight

There are so many different expectations that we as a society place on each other and in turn we place on ourselves — to be the most caring friend, fearless leader, innovative business owner, loving mother or father, passionate lover, amazing cook and incredible housekeeper.

Did society set in stone these perceived rules of behaviour, or is it pressure that we are unintentionally (and unnecessarily) putting on ourselves? Falling into the trap of pleasing others, conforming to societal ideals and being all things to all people can be, if nothing else, totally draining and exhausting. Is the cacophony of voices telling you how you should behave really conducive to leading yourself and others with authenticity?

'Toughen up. Hard work. No play. Don't show vulnerability at work. Make those tough decisions, and now,' says the prototypical fearless leader.

It's time to put a stop to this incessant noise that drowns out dreams, thoughts and opinions, and create a new perspective: to make our own behaviour authentic and honest. It's time to:

- appreciate that each and every one of us is unique
- acknowledge what we are good at and where, quite frankly, we suck
- grab that leadership baton and stand in your spotlight — be a leader who is brave, honest and authentic.

Being authentic benefits everyone. Why? Because, as opposed to the exhaustion of keeping up with how you think you should behave, you accept who you are.

Start promoting yourself. Don't be afraid to emphasise your strengths, what you add in terms of value — and most importantly, your point of difference. In an authentic, realistic way, tell the world what makes you unique. Use what sets you apart as an effective marketing tool.

The business landscape is rapidly evolving and you need to make sure that you are evolving with it. Don't be afraid to self-promote because, when it comes down to it, who knows your message best? You. And much as it is important to be there for those who will be there for you as your business grows, it's time to slap on the greasepaint and get ready to step into your own spotlight. There is nothing wrong with making your own profile, or your own brand, as strong as you possibly can. Because it is only when you are operating from that position of leadership that you can truly give to other people. It is in fact the opposite of selfish to want to achieve your goals — it is self-care.

With that comes energy, excitement and happiness. Step into your own spotlight and be 5 per cent braver than everyone else. Dig deep and share your unique talent, your thought leadership, your expertise; create energy, and that energy will drive change.

Don't be afraid to be brilliant. Have the resilience to shine and follow your dreams of business and personal success. In the poem *Return to Love* Marianne Williamson says that it is not the darkness that frightens us — and it is true. There is a natural human tendency to play down our strengths so that others don't feel insecure around us. She goes on to say when we play small it doesn't serve the world. If we want to be successful in business as well as in life, if we want to collaborate with others to future-proof our success, we have to be okay with being all that we can be and make no apologies for that.

Mandy Holloway, co-founder of Courageous Leaders and author of *Inspiring Courageous Leaders* talks about the pendulum swing effect as people move from protecting themselves and their identity (the space we reference as 'Me') while engaging (the space we reference as 'We') as they swing from behaviour perceived as loyal to that perceived as betrayal. She argues that we have so much untapped potential waiting to be unleashed and, to free this potential, we have to trust each other and collaborate. This requires our leaders to be brave:

> ... to have the courage to have the conversations they fear most; courage to make decisions they would rather delay; courage to address the conflict they have been ignoring and courage to be true in all their actions—true to the leader they want to be and to the kind of organisation all stakeholders want them to build.

Here Mandy discusses the ideology of betrayal and loyalty as it can be applied to the pendulum.

The pendulum of betrayal and loyalty

Higher education institutions globally are teaching young people to bring individual accountability to their learning and interdependence to its application. The result? People want organisations to 'do the right thing' as they seek the following:

- reconnection
    - with a more meaningful and purpose-filled life
    - with other people in their business and personal lives
    - with projects and work that make a holistic difference.
- responsibility
    - at a personal, community and organisational 'soul' level
- revelation
    - of the truth—the whole truth and nothing but the truth!

(continued)

95

The pendulum of betrayal and loyalty *(cont'd)*

People are increasingly demanding trust and seeking collaboration. People are challenging leaders to stay true to the soul of the business and ensure it is not just about chasing the mighty dollar. Business needs to be about so much more than shareholder value and growing the personal wealth of leaders.

Too many of our current business leaders are mesmerised by measurable bottom-line results. The rhetoric about values and culture is not enough to transcend the waves of change.

The current status quo in business blocks the energetic waves of movement and prevents trust and collaboration. People stick with personal agendas when engaging in conversations, when participating in meetings and when making decisions. They are fearful of exposing their real thoughts and needs, as they don't want to lose something or feel threatened. Instead they arrive and engage with a strong Me focus.

So what we currently experience is businesspeople swinging from one end of the pendulum to the other (see figure 6.1) because they lack the courage to bring their core to We-focused conversations. They lack the courage to stay true to their core and tell the truth. Instead the fear of possible loss when working with others gets in the way and they swing from loyalty to betrayal. After all, they have a reputation and results to protect!

Figure 6.1: the pendulum of betrayal and loyalty

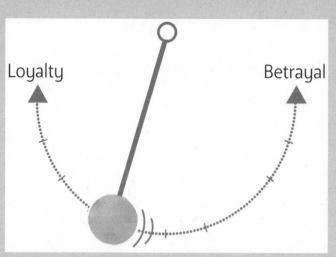

Source: Mandy Holloway.

So what does this pendulum swing look and feel like? People sit in meetings and decide it's best to display 'loyalty' by going with the flow, not rocking the boat, staying with the status quo and being seen as a loyal team member.

The betrayal happens after the meeting when they walk out and talk behind their colleagues' backs, voice disagreement with decisions and blame others for the actions resulting from the meeting.

Or what sometimes happens is someone courageously speaks up in the meeting to challenge the status quo. And because 'challenging' has not been defined as constructive business behaviour they feel the wrath of others for seemingly betraying their colleagues and the accepted norm of behaviour. They leave fearing retribution and the judgement resulting from their actions.

ReConnect Principle 1 is all about bravery as a critical starting point and building belief in Me. The journey towards effective collaboration is overlaying the self-belief with the courage to shift positively and confidently from Me to We.

Case study—volatility versus stability: having the bravery to evolve and succeed

Henry Roth is somewhat of a ubiquitous name in the Australian bridal industry. Known for his meticulous service standards and personal attention to all of his customers (they all have his mobile number to call any time—and it really is any time), Henry has built up an international design empire on the back of his parents' traditional tailoring business. As a former mentor on *Project Runway* and television fashion guru, his stance on the need to be daring in a volatile and uncertain retail economic climate has won him much criticism from bridal industry traditionalists, but he stands by both his service standards and his position on the future of the sector.

Henry and his sister Michelle are currently taking the Henry Roth/Michelle Roth partnership in a very different direction here and in the US. Henry explains how the industry has undergone a complete revolution in the past five years—and what it will face from online competition and an increasingly savvy consumer—and why collaboration with internal and external customers is increasingly essential.

The history of Henry and Michelle Roth's international bridal design success story has its roots firmly planted in the past. Two incredibly tenacious Holocaust survivors—Henry's parents, Aneta and Joseph Weinrich—found freedom and a new beginning in Australia, and re-created a family business in Surry Hills. Aneta and Joseph's drive, determination and ethical way of doing business were instilled in their daughter, Michelle, and son, Henry, who worked in tandem to make a small family design studio into an international phenomenon. A phenomenon, says Henry, that had until recently still followed a market-sensitive, highly traditional business model, with five main tenets at its heart:

- always being highly competitive on a price basis
- never being caught in a style void due to 'creative egos' at the cost of commercial retailability
- never compromising on fit and cut
- providing cutting-edge style without avant-garde attitude
- giving individual, personalised service from the core of the family unit through to exceptional team members in-house, and a vibrant, responsive retail network in Australia, the US, Canada and Hong Kong.

Historically, knowledge within the industry had indicated the following:

- Brides won't buy wedding gowns online.
- They are prepared to be upsold to if they fall in love with an over-budget gown.
- They must have a personal in-store experience.
- The dress comes above any other wedding priority.

Enter 2012—and reality strikes. Brides *are* buying successfully online, at hugely cut prices, from China, and via US designer sample-sale portals. In-store experience was irrelevant as long as the dress was on the money—because every dollar was starting to count. The designer to manufacturer/wholesale to retail model, which created so many fashion success stories—and sent Henry Roth soaring—was no longer viable. And the Roths felt the tangible impact of consumers' new savvy competence in bypassing retail purchases. Significantly. Says Henry:

> We were acutely aware, as a business, and as a family, that fashion on a retail level in Australia was rapidly becoming one of the most dramatically affected industries in the country. When David Jones and Myer are talking mergers ...

you know there is a fundamental shift in the retail landscape that is permanent.

They had a choice; and it was a case of facing the fear and doing it anyway. It was about bravery, and kicking off any traces of artifice:

We as a family business determined that within the tsunami of change, somewhere, somehow, business was being conducted successfully—and it wasn't the government's responsibility to get us that new formula. It was for us to be informed and educated on the new reality and come up with a creative, innovative, risky and above all brave all-or-nothing change.

It was a combination of family pride, tradition ... and ethical principles ... but irrespective of what we did, we knew that the current formula—that traditional business model—was having its last curtain call.

For Henry Roth, the traditional bridal gown business—supplying only to retail—was about to enter a new incarnation.

A bridal factory outlet. Interactive experiences that made the experience memorable and special—dance music, a beauty bar, a barista, an in-house wedding cake designer—but with the dresses at outlet prices. They also engaged with interactive social media platforms and, against all industry norms, launched an online outlet store. The bridal factory outlet was launched in October 2013, on Joseph and Aneta's 60th wedding anniversary.

The truth is ... my parents had an unaccustomed fear that although change was absolutely necessary, their feeling of understanding what we proposed, and the message it may send to our retail base was foreign and truthfully frightening.

Let there be no illusions that we knew in a sober mien, that no change was not an option, and that this 360-degree turnabout in our way of doing business was taking a huge leap of faith with no guarantees of success or consumer acceptance.

What is astounding is the collaborative aspect of the Henry Roth business, because this is where it could have all fallen down, and fallen down badly.

They still have a strong retail base. It is harmonious and non-competitive. All at Henry Roth are upfront and transparent in their dealings with their retail network, and they have been careful to ensure the difference between the outlet store and the retail business. Gowns at outlet are of course not current, there may be irregularities; they are photographed differently and there is no campaign surrounding them. It has kept the retailers understanding that the outlet is not competing with them.

Henry says that it is too early yet to know whether the outlet store (and the coming online business) will deliver the amount of volume necessary to fill the dramatic economic gap made by retailers' shrinking orders, but they have at least assessed that the Australian consumer:

- is completely educated and informed about what they want when they shop

- has an unprecedented number of shopping options that they know how to exercise

- has an almost 'Ned Kelly'–style attitude, built up over decades, that they, as the Australian consumer, have been ripped off through higher prices imposed on goods and services in store

- will question the price and discuss what the final price may be.

Henry says:

> … unless the consumer feels that there is an incredibly good reason for them to abandon their keyboard, they are not going to come in store. If you don't deliver, be prepared for the entire experience — and your business — to collapse. Custom, personalised service is an essential weapon and transparent guarantees of service, quality and accessibility will set you apart — online and in the real world.

Henry Roth. A traditional business now flying in the face of industry practice because its owners have faced the new reality—and acted with bravery. They are prepared to collaborate, to connect, and to cooperate—both with their retailers and, most importantly, with the customer.

Ultimately, for Henry:

> ... regardless of the ultimate capacity of the company to withstand transition, the last six months have been the most professionally rewarding and exciting of my life; instead of being fearful and gridlocked by change, we have embraced it completely, and the interactions we have had with consumers are not just priceless, they have given me a completely new perspective and respect for one of the toughest economic climates I have experienced since I was born in 1960.

> Whether you are a small family business or a behemoth like DJs, we all have one thing in common: the days of thinking 'this is new and fresh' equalling 'you have arrived and can be complacent' are over. The speed of consumer voraciousness means put on your tap shoes, because there's hot coals out there.

Checklist — ReConnect Principle 1: Be Brave

This is your first act of moving from Me to We. Remember — bravado is being shown the door. In order to make the journey from Me to We, you must be brave, be courageous, be yourself and step into your own unique spotlight. Key questions to ask yourself are:

☑ Are you being brave?

☑ Are you taking control of your actions?

☑ Are you living by your own unique value system?

☑ Are you engaging in outside learning?

☑ Are you being open and transparent?

☑ Are you approaching projects with a collaborative mindset?

☑ Are you prepared to take risks?

☑ Are you speaking out?

☑ Are you engaging with others?

☑ Are you disrupting the status quo?

☑ Are you standing in your own spotlight?

chapter 7

ReConnect Principle 2— Build a diverse network

> Sometimes, idealistic people are put off the whole business of networking as something tainted by flattery and the pursuit of selfish advantage. But virtue in obscurity is rewarded only in Heaven. To succeed in this world you have to be known to people.
>
> — *Sonia Sotomayor, Associate Justice of the US Supreme Court*

A powerful network can become your lifeline and is an absolute must-have for successful collaboration.

'Networking' is a term that fills some with the excitement of possibility, some with a sense of absolute dread and others — probably the majority of us — with a combination of feelings: the 'I really don't want to but I know I must' crowd.

Networking, connecting, meeting, doing coffee, lunch dates and even speed connecting — all these terms are synonymous with meeting others to drive skill sets, contacts and ongoing business and personal growth. And however much you might want to hide under the white tablecloths of a corporate breakfast, powerful and effective networking has evolved and is now a business must for all who want to forge ahead. It's not simply about building up a Rolodex of business cards (or, more accurately, a smartphone full of virtual ones), a mass of LinkedIn contacts or a significant number of social media followers. It's about a true meeting of minds and skill sets, and skilfully parlaying said meetings into long-range successful relationships.

Networking is a must-have for successful collaboration, and diversity of that network is the tipping point between average connections and those that collaborate to create magic. The cross-fertilisation of connections, skills and brainpower, and the ideas that are openly discussed and shared through network creation, in their turn create new opportunities, innovation and new solutions to existing problems. It's a domino effect — the way your initial networks interact provides a guideline for the subsequent or flow-on networks that spring up from these collaborations. They will only benefit from your experience and way of working together.

Building a powerful network

In this incredibly fast-paced business and economic landscape we can no longer do it alone — realistically, we never could, we just thought we could. How many times have you heard 'It's not what you know, it's who you know'? Evidence from careercoaching.com.au suggests that in Australia and the US, 70 per cent of executive-level jobs are obtained without formal advertising.

Effective networking is a fundamental part of collaboration. The most innovative businesses and organisations are finding that collaboration and effective and powerful networking are giving them an edge. Do the maths: 'I know one hundred people, they each know one hundred people ...' suddenly, the pyramid is built within an hour of someone mentioning they needed somewhere flash to store some sarcophagi. With technology, six degrees of separation become more like 0.002 degrees.

So how do you find, build and manage a diverse network? How do you gain entry to a true circle of excellence that will work with you and not against you? Because, let's face it, there are still ladder-kickers out there.

Avoid the underminers

Remember when you were at school, and there was always that one friend who seemed absolutely wonderful, but was actually constantly undermining you behind your back? You probably defended them to the death, until one day it hit home that they really were bad news. And so you sought other friends: people of worth who would catch you when you fell, rather than secretly saw through the rungs of your ladder.

This same schoolyard mindset of ladder kickers and the not-so-secret whisperers is still prevalent in the corporate community. In this day and age — when collaborative thinking should be the key not only to success, but to personal growth — this is not the path forward.

Make it diverse

The critical element of a powerful network that can become your lifeline, and is an absolute must-have for successful collaboration, is diversity.

Building an effective and powerful network is so much more than finding a safe like-minded tribe. It requires:

- diversity
- a width and breadth of contacts
- a willingness to embrace the opportunity that exists in differences
- an understanding that you may not always agree with or understand certain points of view, but that through the connection you build awareness and knowledge.

An effective network is a diverse network that consists of people with differing levels of:

- expertise
- age
- gender
- experience.

Powerful networks are those that are cross functional and cross industry. Think about it. A like-minded network limits the breadth of conversation. Lawyers sit in a room with lawyers sharing their legal experience from the industry of law. CEOs play golf with CEOs, fashion industry PR experts mingle with other fashion industry PR experts. Imagine the colour of the conversation if instead you had lawyers, accountants, creatives, athletes, marketers and business owners discussing the various solutions to a problem. Imagine the different perspectives shared, the varying insights, the depth of conversation that would stretch thinking and push perspective wider.

Diverse connections:

- challenge thinking
- drive further questions
- push boundaries
- increase awareness
- open our eyes to another way
- bring to the forefront opportunities that were previously not in the direct line of vision
- present solutions that were not previously on the radar
- create innovations that were once not thought possible.

Get out of the comfort zone

To build a powerful and diverse network involves a willingness to step out of the comfort zone, because comfort zones are anti-growth, breed laziness and limit potential. Dig deep and step out of the place of familiarity and safety to connect with people outside your traditional circle of excellence. It's about making a conscious decision to explore other networks, other people and businesses. Consciously consider who else you could learn from, add value to, engage and collaborate with. It's about:

- attending events that have different groups of people
- talking to someone from a different industry

- debating with people of differing seniority and from differing departments

- engaging with anyone and everyone knowing that we can always learn something.

This absolutely is easier said than done — it takes courage, self-belief and confidence.

Know your goal

An essential part of building a powerful network is understanding what you are seeking to achieve your goal. Now this is not about entering a networking event with a single-minded view of take, take, take, as shown in figure 4.2 (on p. 57). Equally, it's not about risking the empathic position in figure 4.2, when you risk energy depletion from continuously giving to others. It is about understanding what skills, contacts, information, knowledge and insight will push you further in the achievement of your goals.

Surround yourself with inspiring people

Who do you need to surround yourself with to inspire you and your business to achieve more? As Jim Rohn said, 'You are the average of the five people you spend the most time with'.

A powerful network is one that consists of people who:

- have similar mindsets but diverse experience

- will stretch thinking and push boundaries

- realise the power of sharing ideas and of coming together

- value-add to each other's businesses through the power of plural perspectives.

Julie Battilana and Tiziana Casciaro share the power of networking and the important role this skill plays in future-proofing business, careers and success in their report 'Network Secrets of Great Change Agents'. What matters most, they conclude, isn't where someone ranks within a company's formal hierarchy but how well that person understands and mobilises the informal networks needed to effect change.

Magic comes when you create the opportunity to share, collaborate and learn. Diverse groups within your network can bring new thinking and new ideas — a new perspective that could shape your business, your vision, your goal to be stronger, more successful, more scalable than you even thought possible.

The give, give, give of networking

Building an effective network quite simply requires a conscious mind shift and attitude change. A shift from thinking about Me, what I will say, how interesting I am and what I can get from this conversation to thinking about We. It's about:

- a change in attitude
- approaching the meeting of each new person with openness to listen and learn
- a willingness to help and to contribute to their business thinking
- making a personal commitment to deliver on any promises and, ultimately, to stay in touch.

Networking is not about just connecting people. It's about connecting people with people, people with ideas, and people with opportunities.

— Michele Jennae, author of *The Connectworker*

Networking is about:

- constantly exploring how you can do the following:
  - contribute to another's success
  - weave connections, knowledge and insight to benefit them.
- having no expectation of anything in return
- a balanced approach to give and take and keeping in touch because you want to, not just when you want something

- togetherness
- emotional collaboration
- commercial collaboration.

Shoes of Prey founders Michael, Jodie and Mike (their story is discussed in chapter 1) understood the strength of networking and sharing advice in the early days of their business. As Jodie Fox says:

> All of the entrepreneurs that we approached, whether they were running $50 million, $100 million or $2 million businesses, found time for us, to answer our emails or to have a coffee or whatever it was, and that was genuinely a huge surprise to me, and something that we try to give back to the community as well.

Jodie advises people to network. 'Don't be afraid to reach out to people and introduce yourself. And now, with access available to most people via social media, there's no reason to be shy.'

Reciprocal networking drives incremental success as individuals constantly look for ways to give and add value to their network. The give, give, give of networking specifically requires:

- willingly offering new information or expertise
- openly sharing best practice
- inspiring innovation
- asking questions
- giving feedback
- actively making connections and introductions
- promoting others' businesses, skills and expertise — opening up doors for others' commercial advantage
- supporting dreams and big-picture visions, sharing insights to add value to those visions.

Be an example to those in your network. Model the behaviour that you seek in return. Give knowledge unconditionally, open doors willingly, share insight to drive continued growth and success for others, attract them and engage because of who you are, your dreams and your actions.

As Richard Branson said, 'Nobody can be successful alone'.

Managing your network

Regular communication — and not just when you need something — is key. It's fundamentally about having an awareness of what your network is looking for — what opportunities you come across — so that sharing will support the achievement of someone else's vision or plan. It's about:

- actively promoting others

- engaging and making connections within and across networks

- driving support and sales opportunities for others

- not expecting anything in return.

Successful management of your network requires 100 per cent delivery on what you say you are going to do and any promises made. Equally it requires you to take on board other people's suggestions. If someone provides a lead, it is important to follow through with that lead. Equally, thank the introducer and provide feedback on the introduction. Now, I am not saying you must do what others say — ultimately you own your decisions and directions — but for a network to work effectively over time it is imperative that you act on the back of recommendations.

Regularly and continuously adding value through communication is integral. Listen to others' dreams and willingly share what you know and who you know to support their dreams.

Be known for you, your value system, integrity and value add; don't be known as someone who continuously takes but doesn't give back.

A word of warning: beware the dream stealers

Dream stealers are the antithesis of being brave, of networking to mutual benefit, of commercially collaborating — and they are everywhere, so beware.

They are the sappers of positivity. The drainers. The ones that don't add constructive thoughts to your business dreams or the collective conversation, but instead actually steal them and snuff them out — or worse, steal them for themselves.

Unfortunately they are often closer than you think: friends, colleagues — even family members — who tell you 'you can't', 'it won't work', 'it isn't safe'. People who encourage you to play it safe because safety is, well, reassuring to them.

But what does it mean for you?

No dreams achieved. Just a nagging feeling of, 'What just happened here?' and knowing that in the name of love, people have just stamped on your ambition and killed it cold.

I do believe that some of these dream stealers genuinely want to protect you and really do think they have your best intentions at heart. But what about those jealous or purely negative dream stealers — the ones that quite simply don't want to see you achieve? What about those who are actively hanging on to revel in your failure?

Dream stealers tend to comment without solicitation, and most of the time negatively. They will subtly put doubt in your mind. They will attempt to erode your confidence in yourself — sometimes because they recognise the brilliance of what you have to share with the world and see an opportunity for themselves.

Are these the type of people to include in your circle of excellence?

Have the courage to open your eyes — open them wide — and walk away from the dream stealers. Instead, dream big and find a diverse network that adds value to your thinking, your business, your dreams.

Become aware of the negative comments that are being shared around you, and instead of listening, choose to block them out and not engage. Instead, find those people who will not only dream with you but will offer constructive advice, input, thought and insight to ensure you are moving forward in the right direction — in your direction.

Your network needs you

ReConnect Principle 2 is essential to support commercial collaboration, as it is all about expanding your thinking and network to attract other experts to your circle of influence, other specialists who can add a level of insight and thought leadership that you quite simply don't have on your own. It's simple — a powerful and diverse network is an essential part of business and personal development. It will ensure that the best opportunities, ideas and talent come your way.

Case study—the standard you walk past

Lieutenant General David Morrison, AO, joined Army in 1979, after completing a Bachelor of Arts at the Australian National University. He rose steadily through the ranks of the military, serving in Papua New Guinea in 1994, and was made a member of the Order of Australia in 1999 for his services as Brigade Major, Director of Preparedness and Mobilisation and as Commanding Officer.

He was promoted to colonel in October 1999 and served as Colonel of Operations in East Timor. His services culminated, after many subsequent promotions, in his 2011 appointment as Chief of Army.

Lieutenant General Morrison has been involved at a frontline level in the reforms of the Australian Defence Force after several high-level incidents involving the unacceptable treatment of women. He is known for his lack of tolerance for those who see themselves as above the law and for his active promotion of women on their merits in the ADF. He is a firm believer in the benefits of collaborative business practices, both in Defence and in the private sector. Here is what he has to say about diversity of collaboration:

> Army and the Australian Defence Force are, by their very nature, not only required to do, think and act in a collaborative manner, but are well aware of the *benefits* of collaboration and of moving from a Me space to a We space. On operations, for example, you are not just collaborating within your team and with your allies from other nations, but with the members of the societies you are there to protect. Collaborative thinking is therefore inherently rooted at an organisational level.
>
> There are very big changes currently occurring at the ADF. We are now harnessing the talent of those individuals who have been largely underrepresented in the past; not just women, but also socio-economic and ethnic groups in Australia who don't see military service as a tradition, and perhaps hadn't been widely encouraged by recruitment campaigns either.
>
> As the current leadership team came into its position of authority in 2011, and as a consequence of serious investigations into the ADF (13 of which were major), there was a recognition for me personally that we as a defence force had not properly addressed the above matters. I call it one of my 'Saul on the road to Damascus' moments, and it came after a conversation with Liz Broderick (Australia's Sex Discrimination Commissioner and Head of the Review into Sexual Discrimination at the Australian Defence Force Academy). We were a part of a systemic problem within society.
>
> It's something I come back to on so many occasions— and it's the first step on turning Me into We within Army and the wider world. Army, the ADF, corporate entities—we

all have our identities. Army has 113 years of an incredibly strong culture. It's our idea of service to the nation, that core matter, that helps us do what we are asked to do. Coming to the conclusion that there were things that were deeply wrong within that culture was very hard. Being deeply committed as a leader, having to say that there's something deeply wrong, and saying that to that body as a whole was incredibly difficult and challenging—but it was something I had to do.

This was particularly clear when, in early 2011, the ADF was subject to intense scrutiny after the ADFA 'Skype' scandal. It was my view initially that the actions of cadets after less than ten weeks within the confines of the Academy was a reflection on their upbringing, rather than on the military, but after a lot of hard thought, I changed my view 180 degrees.

Why? Because our culture has habitually excluded rather than included. I refer to what I call the 'ANZAC myth'. The ANZACS have become almost a caricature; we have begun to see ourselves as the best soldiers in the First World War—male Anglo-Saxons who didn't have to do much to win, who didn't salute, didn't respect their superiors, who fought best with a hangover. As a result, some members of today's army and ADF see themselves as so-called 'natural warriors'—and those outside these parameters will struggle for recognition if they are not the embodiment of this. They are never going to realise their natural talents if a culture of exclusion persists.

Today's ADF works in very challenging environments and ethnically diverse ones, with threatened and frightened men and women. If we haven't built a force to be inclusive and value diversity, it is clearly not going to be as effective, because those in a position of weakness and vulnerability won't respond to those who represent the 'ANZAC myth'.

This moment of clarity brought a realisation that we weren't as capable as we needed to be, and reinforced for the ADF the value of going from Me to We and being inclusive. Through harnessing talent we will achieve truly groundbreaking development. And this is the great journey that Army has been on for the last three years.

This is the initiative that I am the most proud of, not personally, but as Chief of Army.

In 2011, women made up less than 10 per cent of our numbers. How much talent and potential was going to waste? These were matters that had to be dealt with. Thankfully there was a unilateral senior-level buy-in from Chief of Defence Force (General David Hurley, AC, DSC), and the other chiefs. Some tremendous initiatives started to be put in place. Unfortunately some abhorrent behaviour came to the fore at this time, and it came from senior officers and non-commissioned men. What it *did* do was put into very sharp focus the leaders' response—that this is simply not good enough—and that those responsible were being held very appropriately to account. It also showed that we knew we had to do better. Men were sacked. Education campaigns were put in place. International attention was attracted—for the right reasons in the end, and deservedly so—but we are not complacent.

We have increased the number of women in Army to 11.7 per cent, but there is still so far to go. We have the best diversity policy in the military world—the best maternity leave, and no loss of seniority after maternity leave. I am involved as a Male Champion of Change, helping to show corporate what we are doing in Army.

This is essential best practice. It's not about a 'fair go', it's not about politically correct objectives. It's about making a 113-year-old body as robust as possible in the 21st century. It's about capability.

An increase of 400 women in three years is a step in the right direction, when these are women who have joined because of merit and capability. We are seeing a dramatic increase in numbers of women coming to Duntroon and soldier training, with numbers now at 16 to 20 per cent.

Having greater diversity at all levels has to be driven from the top, and to recognise talent in a less traditional way—that's the biggest challenge that any organisation has.

For me, if Army isn't a We, how do you lay claim to being an army? How do you lay claim to defending a nation? We are the protectors of that nation—not an organisation or a culture of Me.

For a defence force in particular, the tone of the culture has to be embraced by everyone in the organisation—but if there is change, you have to make them aware of the reasons for the need for change. And yes, there are always recalcitrants—but in today's army, and today's culture, those who are not prepared to embrace thoughtful change and diversity are out.

For me, it's as simple as this: the standard you walk past is the standard you are prepared to accept.

Case study—collaborating the old with the new

The Australian Museum faced two firsts in 2014. The nation's oldest museum has appointed the first non-scientist as its director to lead the institution—and the first female.

Their choice was, at first glance, highly unconventional. Kim McKay, AO, was new not only to a scientific environment but also to the Australian public service, a challenge in itself for someone unused to bureaucracy in its most rarefied form. But this is a woman who understands not only how to work her way through the machinations of institutions with little fuss and bother, but also how people work. She embodies the power of networking at its finest in terms of making it work for oneself, and in turn, benefiting others in the same circles. They gain from her incredible intelligence, charisma, humour and blunt up-front approach to problem solving.

In 1989, Kim McKay co-founded the Clean Up Australia organisation with solo yachtsman Ian Kiernan, which today is one of the largest community environmental projects in the world, annually attracting over half a million volunteers. This was expanded in 1992 to Clean Up the World, for which she secured partnership with the United Nations Environment Programme and international corporate support. She has worked for the Discovery Channel and National Geographic Channels International in the US, and was the director of Momentum2, a social marketing and communications consultancy, prior to being named the director of the Australian Museum. She managed the media and publicity for Oprah's tour of Australia as well as ongoing work for Oprah's production company, Harpo Productions.

She is an author, media commentator and award winner as well as holder of the Order of Australia.

But many people are authors, media commentators, television personalities, directors of companies — what is it about Kim McKay that makes her the embodiment of ReConnect Principle 2?

It's simple. She has an innate ability to:

- promote
- engage
- promulgate interest
- communicate.

She listens to what those around her want to achieve, and she makes it happen through matching their needs with those of their audiences. She did it for Oprah Winfrey and Jessica Watson, and she did it for the Discovery Channel and the National Geographic Channel through cable television. She has raised millions for philanthropic causes, again through matching the right people with the right backing. She is open and frank about the need for the Australian Museum to gain new funding, and that this is part of her role as director—and part of the role of all senior staff, whether they have experience in this arena or not. As she says:

> I think it's a reality that all cultural institutions are run in a slightly different way than they were run previously. There's no doubt that the director role is now the CEO role of the organisation.

> I would never pretend to be a scientist and sit down in a lab here, but nor should I, because I've got so many other things to do. You are like a producer, in a way. You are looking for where the money is coming from. You are looking for the best talent to bring on board to manage things. You are looking for how you communicate effectively to your audience.

It is this bluntness that has seen her be castigated by some. And this is true of most powerful networkers. You can, to paraphrase Abraham Lincoln, never please all of the people all of the time. It is doubtful whether it bothers her, considering the success she has achieved, not just for herself but for the institutions and individuals she has been involved with and worked for. Again, this is the key to successful networking—being more engaged in the success of others than your own.

When interviewed by The Australian on the announcement of her appointment to the museum—and it was a controversial appointment—outgoing director Frank Howarth summed up why she will be a success:

> It's a very good appointment at this point in the museum's history. The museum is about to embark on major changes … and it's a time when museums everywhere need to be more outwardly focused, to communicate better.

He also praised McKay's 'incredible background in philanthropy', saying her lack of formal science qualifications doesn't matter, as it's more important that his successor has 'capital-L leadership skills and ability to look outside the museum, build its influence and build the museum's profile'.

Networking brought the Australian Museum its new director. In many ways, the museum needs a new approach: revenue has been down, funding has been cut and visitor numbers have thinned dramatically. Can a woman, a non-scientist, someone from a collaborative, 21st-century business methodology, bring an almost extinct beast back to viability?

In her role, Kim McKay connects thought and opportunity, travelling the world forging partnerships with others such as the Natural History Museum, the State Hermitage Museum and the Smithsonian Institution in Washington. If Kim McKay's network supports her as she has supported them then the answer has to be yes.

Checklist — ReConnect Principle 2: Build a diverse network

The power of a diverse network is absolutely undeniable in future-proofing your success and your career. Judicious, collaborative networking can mean the difference between a business expanding successfully or going backwards. Learning how to network well is a skill that takes you from a closed mindset to an open business model that leads to long-term benefits for both yourself and your networking partners — commercial collaboration at play.

Make sure you look closely at the following:

☑ Who are you currently networking with and can this circle be expanded to include more diversity?

☑ What value can you share with your network?

☑ What value are they adding to you?

☑ Do you openly ask for help and support?

☑ Would you be likely to engage with these people outside of a networking event?

☑ Is there a level of trust?

☑ Would you be willing and happy to cross-promote your network's businesses through your own platforms without hesitation?

☑ Do you feel they are open to collaborative thinking?

☑ Do you have similar ethical standards?

☑ Is there a conflict of interest with your businesses?

☑ Who is not adding value to you within your current network?

☑ Do you regularly check in with your network, and not just when you want something?

chapter 8

ReConnect Principle 3— Full disclosure

> Seldom, very seldom, does complete truth belong to any
> human disclosure; seldom can it happen that something
> is not a little disguised, or a little mistaken.
>
> — *Jane Austen, author*

**Commercial collaboration will not be successful unless
there is full disclosure — of strengths, skills, talent, goals and
successes alongside openly sharing threats and weaknesses.**

Full disclosure strengthens ReConnect Principle 2, your
powerful network, and supports individuals and businesses
owning their Me space, standing comfortably and confidently
in the knowledge of their skills, expertise and big-picture goals.
At the same time, and this is the tricky one for many, it includes
the hidden and previously untapped skills of:

- showing vulnerability

- having the courage to speak up and stand in your own spotlight

- facing fears

- learning from failure.

Individuals and leaders who disclose fully, who are authentic
and engage others allow others to become more. As author
Simon Sinek said in his TED talk 'Why good leaders make you
feel safe': 'If you get the environment right every single one of us

has the capacity to do remarkable things'. Sinek says that belief, trust and cooperation are created when people feel safe; and remarkable things happen when leaders make their team feel safe. This is such a key element of commercial collaboration. It is the space of diverse connection and facilitating contribution that benefits the organisation. If people feel safe they seize the opportunity to evolve, do more, disrupt and innovate, to try and fail.

Full disclosure is about being open to the opportunity that exists on the other side of the comfort zone. This principle discusses the ways you can embrace both fear and vulnerability without losing your business direction — and without opening yourself up to the point where you are actually unprofessional.

Vulnerability is a strength

Owning our story can be hard but not nearly as difficult as spending our lives running from it. Embracing our vulnerabilities is risky but not nearly as dangerous as giving up on love and belonging and joy — the experiences that make us the most vulnerable. Only when we are brave enough to explore the darkness will we discover the infinite power of our light.

— Brené Brown, author of *The Gifts of Imperfection*

We all know the 'hard' skills needed to be successful at work, the ones necessary to do our jobs as well as we can — and it doesn't matter whether they have been learned through education, mentorship or simply from doing. Leading. Managing a team. Being able to forecast trends. Budgeting. Meeting KPIs. All these skills are invaluable.

But perhaps there is another essential element to success. Something we've chosen to ignore and in fact see as a weakness in the business arena. It's a skill that:

- takes courage and strength
- can become the most powerful part of our armour, instead of the chink that people expect it to be

- surprises some, warms you to others and takes people off guard
- puts you in the moment, on the ball and in a position to create magic and genius.

It is a skill that, to totally generalise, men very rarely show. It is a skill that women, for whatever reason, have (again to generalise) forgotten, thrown out, or simply pushed away.

It is vulnerability. Sound scary? You're lying, or at least not thinking fully about it, if you say no.

Vulnerability is scary and sometimes uncomfortable. Even at times almost uncontrollable. But — and this is a very, very big but — it is also incredibly powerful.

Vulnerability is:

- an essential skill for successful leaders
- part of being able to be open and transparent
- a necessary element in working collaboratively — because how can one work with full disclosure if parts of a personality are being withheld?

We have been ingrained with the concept that in business (and sometimes in life) vulnerability is a weakness, because it is sharing openly your thoughts and fears; it is allowing others to see your true self. It is speaking your truth.

But vulnerability should be seen as powerful. Herein lies the opportunity:

- for collaboration
- to create a small ripple, a change of light, a change of thought in someone else's thinking
- to trigger a new thought process.

We are too scared to share our feelings. This is a parlous state of affairs. What you think, what your intuition is telling you, and being able to articulate the two, equals the chance to more easily move forward.

By sharing our thoughts, our feelings, our worries and our concerns we actually open the door to:

- change
- let others in
- gain support
- meet new people
- try new experiences
- develop a new way of thinking.

Why shouldn't this display of 'vulnerability' equal power and strength, rather than weakness?

Vulnerability embraces boundaries and trust. Being vulnerable does take courage to:

- quiet the mind
- share our thoughts, feelings and opinions honestly
- connect with others who have earned the right to hear our stories.

If you have the strength to be vulnerable and show your true self within business, what an incredible gift and model this is to others.

Keep the hard skills, because without them, you don't have a business. But allow yourself to be the one thing that is most necessary to succeed in the long run. And above anything else, it means you are conquering something so enormous it is hardly discussed openly — fear.

It is of course impossible to talk about the 'power' of vulnerability without mentioning academic Brené Brown. Her TED talk from 2010 on the power of vulnerability has been viewed more than 15 200 000 times, and in 2013 she published *Daring Greatly*.

'Vulnerability is not weakness,' writes Brown. In fact, 'vulnerability is the core, the heart, the centre of meaningful human experiences'.

Dr Brown started seeing a therapist after a breakdown — and before that cheerfully admits that she saw vulnerability as a weakness. Now, it is essential to living a 'wholehearted' life; and the workplace is absolutely a part of this. To lead, one has to admit one is vulnerable — how can a person be whole without some form of 'realness'? It is what makes us human and connects us. This is the key to our relationships with others, and goes back to the storytelling point; telling your story involves others in your journey, and encourages them to want to be part of it.

'Vulnerability is the absolute heartbeat of innovation and creativity,' says Brown. 'There can be zero innovation without vulnerability.'

Or, perhaps in the words of John Steinbeck, 'Now that you don't have to be perfect, you can be good'.

There is a difference, however, between being vulnerable and letting everything out at once — lock, stock and barrel. There are still levels of what is appropriate to the workplace and what isn't. So how do we define what should come out and what should stay buried in the filing cabinets of our subconscious permanently?

Tell your story

Depending on the size of your company, it may be just management that you share your story with — but let them know who you are. Share what is going on. Make them a part of your journey. This is not a 'let me tell you what I had for breakfast this morning' tale, but more where you see the company is going, what you feel you are doing to raise the company's profile, where you would like assistance.

Involve others in the decision-making process

Are you trying to make all the decisions yourself and failing miserably because every day doesn't have 62 hours in it—and because one person shouldn't have *all* the answers in their head? (If that were the case, what do you even need a team for?) The reason you employ specialists is because they are specialists. Admit that you are not an engineer if you're not an engineer. Same goes if you're not the company lawyer. This is not even about being vulnerable; it's about being sensible. Sometimes we get so twisted up in proving ourselves that we forget that no-one is everything to everyone. Let others prove their worth. You may find that they are feeling vulnerable too because they are concerned they are not making their own mark, or having enough input. Don't lose valuable members of a team through being SuperBoss.

Don't ignore the elephant in the room

Vulnerability is not something that will ever go away. It is a part of you just as much as your hair colour or whether or not you like red wine. Try to ignore it, and it will be at your peril. To declare oneself invulnerable would be inauthentic and would leave a leader living in a perpetual state of denial and stress. So it's better and more courageous for every leader to acknowledge the fact that vulnerability is there.

You have a voice—use it

We all have a choice; and that choice is not just about passion and dynamism. Full disclosure involves:

- speaking up
- sharing your opinions, ideas, thoughts, strengths
- asking for help where support is needed.

It's about living and breathing your brand, disclosing who you are, your value system and your beliefs. It's your voice; use it.

Your opinion matters, your views are unique to you, your voice is your gift to share and you matter.

Whether we are paving our own entrepreneurial life, following our corporate career dream, raising a family or continually learning to be the best we can be, the impact that we have on those immediately around us is significant and should never be underestimated.

Every action we take and word we speak adds to the full disclosure bucket — our own perception of what we want to show passion for, and the perception of others in terms of how they both benefit from and give back to our passion.

We are all in this together. Your success is there to be created if you collaborate openly, willingly and with complete, honest and full disclosure. You have the ability to influence one to one, many to many, more to more — your team, your colleagues, your leaders, your children, their friends, your friends and your family. But it needs you to speak up.

Too often people sit back and say nothing when something needs to be said. They may have an idea, a viewpoint that contradicts the masses or an insight that will add to the group thought — but instead of speaking up they keep quiet.

Why is this? Fear? Lack of confidence? Concern about upsetting others?

The reality is that by not speaking up you are not being the Me that you are supposed to be. You are not bringing Me into the space of We, the space of commercial collaboration. You are not leaning in, being brave, having the courageous conversation, contributing to the collaborative experience. Above all you are not creating the space to gift your knowledge, thoughts, opinions or expertise to others. You are not enabling an opportunity for others to listen, learn and add to your thought process. By staying silent you may end up being a detrimental influence on the very people or group you don't wish to harm.

Your experience and knowledge are unique to you and as such, your thoughts have as much value in a situation as others. To quote Vera Nazarian, author of *The Duke in His Castle*:

> Yawns are not the only infectious things out there besides germs. Giggles can spread from person to person. So can blushing. But maybe the most powerful infectious thing is the act of speaking the truth.

Failure is an opportunity to learn

Inventor James Dyson went through 5127 prototypes and 5126 'failures' to get his massively successful vacuum cleaner right. Five thousand, one hundred and twenty-seven — but he got there. This is the stuff of legend — and the difference between active and passive vulnerability for an entrepreneur. Passive vulnerability means being vulnerable without choosing to be. Active? In essence, it's informed and proactive risk-taking, admitting that you know there is an incredibly high risk of failure, but being willing to let yourself be exposed, because there is a chance it will pay off. This is not just emotional vulnerability, but also financial vulnerability, but it springs from the same place: taking a chance and allowing yourself to commit 100 per cent, to let others see all of you.

Imagine if Dyson had said 'Nope, I give up' after prototype 5125? He was fond of saying that the entrepreneur's life was one of failure — but he still kept going. That is vulnerability at its finest, and true leadership.

> *There are no secrets to success. It is the result of preparation, hard work, and learning from failure.*

— General Colin Powell, former US Secretary of State

There is an extremely practical and no-nonsense book by Siimon Reynolds called *Why People Fail*. In it, Reynolds says how important it is that we give both our staff, and ourselves as leaders, permission to fail, because it leads to incredibly valuable lessons.

How often do we allow ourselves the luxury — and it is regarded by 99 per cent of us as a luxury — of seeing so-called 'failure' as a learning experience, and therefore a positive, rather than a negative that we spend hours, days — sometimes years — beating ourselves up about?

In our work history, how often have we experienced that sick-to-the-stomach, 'Oh God I am a dead man/woman walking' feeling as we slowly drag our heels to the boss's office, ready to hear the words, 'I'm sorry, but this is just too big a mistake to ignore — you're going to have to face [fill in worst-case scenario]'?

If you can honestly say 'never', then chances are you haven't pushed yourself to the brink of your capability. Because true leaders stuff up. They make mistakes. They fail — sometimes catastrophically. Jack Welch, who eventually became CEO of General Electric, literally exploded a fairly large area of a plant as a lowly line manager. But it is how he grew from that experience that made him the powerhouse leader that he eventually became.

Failure is a chance to regroup, learn and grow. As leaders and business owners it is our duty to ensure that others in the workforce, coming up through the ranks, don't end up bowed and bloodied by mistakes that they make.

Full disclosure is about sharing what you've learned with others. It is important that failures are embraced as a learning opportunity, a chance to see what was wrong with a method, or an approach — or even an experiment, Mr Welch! — and improve on it. To guide and give support, not scream and rant and punish but add to thinking to avoid a repeat of the same mistake. In its place will be a shared lesson that adds to the achievement of someone else's goal.

Turn fear into success

Sometimes what we are most afraid of is success — so we turn inwards, and keep our ideas to ourselves. If we don't succeed, we can blame it on others and not ourselves, because it is others' ideas and innovations that have been presented and not our own. If we are the ones at the top of the tree, this is both unfair and unnatural. The fear cycle has to be broken, and it needs to be broken through openness and transparency, and a willingness to put ideas and vision out there.

'You're the head honcho,' says Linda Sapadin, a US-based psychologist and author of *Master Your Fears*, 'so you really need to be able to get beyond the fear in order to make your business happen.'

Sapadin likes to invoke the example set by the Cowardly Lion, the spineless (but ultimately heroic) character created by L. Frank Baum in the book *The Wonderful Wizard of Oz*. 'People think having courage means you have no fear,' Sapadin says. 'Courage is taking action despite the fear.' In other words, fear means go.

Bill Gates. Steve Jobs. Mark Zuckerberg. All three didn't complete university. Why? Because they were willing to face and overcome their fear of failure and look towards what they truly wanted — to rock the boat and ultimately succeed. Bill Gates has actually said 'failure is a great teacher'. They were, and are, future focused, and willing to fail because of that focus. This is why they have succeeded where others have failed — because others have allowed the fear to overcome them.

On the flip side are the examples of brands that didn't embrace ReConnect Principle 3 to disclose fully and learn from failures. Kodak, Atari, Blockbuster — all are examples of businesses that looked to the past and didn't collaborate. They stayed inward-looking, focusing on Me, instead of taking the opportunity to seek help and collaborate in the We space.

ReConnect Principle 3 involves full disclosure and the acknowledgement of fear as opposed to hiding it behind a protective barrier. Embracing fear requires:

- honesty
- authenticity
- courage
- vulnerability
- facing it head on
- exploring ways to overcome it
- resilience
- a belief in the bigger picture
- a sheer determination to keep pursuing the vision for a sustainable future.

Everyone experiences fear. And to be vulnerable — to openly share, ask for help, admit what you don't know or even what you love with no knowledge of whether there will be reciprocity — is power.

Full disclosure involves understanding the fear:

- Is it a healthy fear, or one that is based purely on your own insecurities and self doubts?
- Is it a valid fear or more about not knowing how to overcome it, not having the answers yet?
- Is it a fear that is serving no purpose to your end goal?
- Is it actually a fear that needs to be dismissed?

Imagine how easy it is to answer these questions about fear if you open up to your network and circle of influence. As the saying goes, 'A problem shared is a problem halved'.

Fear:

- is a gift
- is a great teacher
- provides a chance to pause, review and regroup
- gives an opportunity to:
  - choose the next path
  - connect the head with the heart
  - engage others
  - determine a new direction and the steps that you need to take.

Facing fear head on, with others, builds strength, resilience and determination. It provides a journey and a shift in perspective.

Case study—full disclosure is exposure; exposure is strength and opportunity.

Carol Yang enjoyed a highly successful (and high flying) corporate career. In 2009, she had an enormous realisation—this wasn't enough. For too long, she had been operating without acknowledging what truly mattered to her. This realisation led her to some scary places, and enormous vulnerability.

It also led her to what has now turned out to be the happiest—and bravest—stage of her working life. She is now the owner of her own life-coaching business, Spring Forward, born out of her own experiences of rediscovery and living authentically.

This is Carol's journey in her own words:

It's 2009 and I'm sitting in my beautiful office looking out at another glorious winter's day in the north-east US. Snow-capped trees glint in the sunlight. In many ways, I'm at the pinnacle of my career—vice-president of global marketing for the Timberland Company, a corporate warrior with her fair share of wins and battle scars. Over two decades of climbing the corporate ladder have paid off. Sure, there was a lot of hard work along the way, but the rewards were equal in measure. It opened up access to thought leaders who inspired me, challenged and enabled me to grow as a person and business leader. I saw the world, albeit often from an aeroplane or the latest boardroom we were in, but saw the world I did. I had the privilege of living and working in Japan, Australia and the US—experiences I would not have traded for anything.

My journey began with Procter & Gamble many moons ago when I was recruited into their marketing department straight out of university. For 13 years I honed my marketing skills in the best marketing and leadership 'school' in the world (okay, so perhaps I'm just a tad biased) and took on ever-greater leadership responsibilities, both regionally and globally. Even then, I had a restlessness. A sense that there was something else for me. A call that I did not yet understand but nonetheless still felt.

I can't help but reminisce about how far I've come, and importantly where I want to go next. For all intents and purposes I had 'everything'—a loving family, great friends, a senior position with a leading global company with strong values, a stimulating job where I could leave my mark; and the peace of mind that comes with financial security. I was doing well and could check items off the traditional list of how success is measured. Really, what else could I ask for?

Yet, why did I have a nagging feeling that it was time to chart a new path? You see, as much as I enjoyed my work and loved Timberland, I felt like something was missing. There had to be more, and I don't mean more money or more status or power. Deep within me, I felt that what defined me as a person—the real, authentic me—was not being fulfilled. I could not see myself continuing down my current path. It wasn't the job or the company. I knew the restlessness was due to a deeper hunger inside me. I could not put it off any longer. I had to resolve this. It was time to take my life to the next level.

Making the decision to leave a successful career with absolutely no idea of what was next was perhaps the most terrifying and liberating thing I've ever done. I will always be grateful to my bosses at Timberland for their support and understanding. To Mike Harrison and Jeff Swartz, my heartfelt thanks and sincere gratitude.

That decision began my journey of self-discovery and personal awakening. The first thing I did was what most of us tend to do—I decided that I was smart enough to figure this out on my own and resisted sharing my dilemmas or seeking advice for fear of looking vulnerable or weak. I was, after all, a strong successful leader who had 'made it'. How could I possibly reveal how confused and conflicted I secretly was? That was my first painful lesson.

I learnt that going it alone when it comes to big, gut-wrenching problems is not the best solution. When I moved past my fear of showing my vulnerability, the fog started to lift. I began to openly share what I was struggling with. I actively sought advice and support from other seasoned executives. I put my strengths to work. To my surprise, I found others who had faced similar crossroads, who were not afraid to share their insights and knowledge and who inspired me through their own journeys.

Through this I've learnt that while full disclosure can leave us uncomfortably exposed, it can also bring inspiration to the surface and find support in the most unexpected places.

And as we share our own challenges and triumphs, we pay it forward to inspire and empower others. I've also learnt to be more comfortable with uncertainty. With not needing to know all the answers before proceeding. I know that fear is to be expected, but that should not stop me from moving ahead anyway. Perhaps most importantly, I've learnt to trust my intuition even as it takes me down unconventional paths.

For those of you feeling stuck at the crossroads, I urge you to pause and reflect on some tough questions. Questions that will help you stay on course with what's truly meaningful to you. And when you do hit a roadblock, lean into your vulnerability and seek advice and support. From experience, I know you will find others who face the same. Remember to listen to both your head and heart. Your intuition is there for a reason.

Fast forward to today. I now have clarity of purpose. I've gotten back in touch with what's truly meaningful and important to me. I will always love building brands. Yet I know that connecting and contributing to individuals on a deeper, more personal level is what fulfils me the most.

Inspired by my personal journey and belief in the power of clarity of purpose, I founded Spring Forward Australia to empower executives who are at a crossroads to create their next path in life. We owe it to ourselves to give ourselves permission to press pause and define what success truly means to us. Like creating a brand, we have to first start with identifying our true essence to begin clarifying our purpose. To live an inspired, purposeful and fulfilling life, authentic to who we truly are.

Checklist — ReConnect Principle 3: Full disclosure

We understand the 'hard skills' needed as leaders. But we also now understand that the 'soft skills' — admitting vulnerability, admitting fear — can also be invaluable. Full disclosure is a part of successful future-proofing. Being able to use our fears — to engage with others through vulnerability — is an essential part of leadership. This is a new way of thinking, a new way of collaborating — a new kind of strength.

How do we make sure that fear and vulnerability are 'used' in the right way in the workplace? How do we make sure, as leaders, that our actions are authentic? How do we make our teams feel safe so that they evolve and innovate, knowing that failure is not an automatic push-to-the-kerb offence?

☑ Acknowledge the fear. What are you afraid of?

☑ Understand the fear. Is it healthy or irrational?

☑ Use it as a gift. Fear means go. Are you rocking the boat?

☑ Tell your story to your team.

☑ Involve your staff in the decision-making process.

☑ Be active, not passive in your vulnerability.

☑ Embrace your vulnerabilities.

☑ Speak up — use your voice.

☑ Learn from your failures.

chapter 9

ReConnect Principle 4—
Disrupt

It's just that if you're not disruptive everything seems to
be repeated endlessly—not so much the good things
but the bland things—the ordinary things—the weaker
things get repeated—the stronger things get suppressed
and held down and hidden.

— *Professor Robert Adamson, Scottish philosopher*

**Disrupters understand the value of not accepting the bland
and the boring.**

Think about any great mind of the past hundred years. Einstein.
Oppenheimer. Margaret Sanger. Logie Baird. Gates. Jobs.
Marissa Mayer.

Every one of these people took the road less travelled, enabled
change and disrupted the status quo.

They were not satisfied with the traditional, the ordinary and
the everyday. They questioned what was in front of them and
tore down the methods, products or ideas that were accepted at
the time and created a new vision. They didn't even accept their
own vision as enough but constantly innovated and sought
new and better ways to do business, find solutions, increase
productivity.

They were disrupters. And they understood the value of not
accepting the bland and the boring.

Where are you accepting average?

In terms of your own leadership style and the way you are working on a day-to-day basis, there are critical questions you need to ask yourself and answer honestly: where are you currently accepting average? What are you tolerating that needs to change?

Perhaps you have been enjoying a period of success. It's easy to slip into that acceptance of the status quo, the comfort zone. This is inward looking and will ultimately mean you will be overtaken by the good leader, the disruptive leader, who constantly looks to the future and asks the questions:

- What's next?

- Where's the risk?

- Who is innovating while we aren't?

- What new technology is around the corner?

Disruption doesn't mean a ruthless approach. It doesn't mean putting pure profit ahead of people and the short-term win ahead of long-term relationships. In fact, in many ways it's just the opposite of this because disrupters have an end-goal vision. They are invariably entrepreneurial and collaborative as opposed to those who operate fully in the Me space, inevitably putting themselves and their business practices inside a box and closing the lid to outside thinking, influences and the possibility of change.

Collaborate and change

Disruption is:

- a willingness to collaborate and change

- doing business with a leading edge

- thinking with agility, not lethargy

- involving your team in the process of change.

Disruptive leaders are incredibly good at recognising that there is always a yin and a yang in every situation in life, and business isn't different. They are open and transparent because this is key to collaborative success. Secrecy is anathema.

The chance to change the rules, to contribute individually and to create disruption is here. The opportunity to change the corporate and business landscape is now — not tomorrow.

Take a moment to look at where you are tolerating average thought — from yourself and from others — and where you could disrupt thinking. Where can your team be disrupters? How can you give them the confidence to engage and overcome the fear of change?

Disruptive innovation

Professor Clayton M. Christensen first coined the term 'disruptive innovation' to describe the phenomenon by which an innovation transforms an existing market or sector by introducing simplicity, convenience, accessibility and affordability where complication and high cost are the status quo. In the same way, those leaders who are willing to transform their businesses by introducing new and simplified procedures, great ideas and great products are disruptive *innovators*.

Apple changed the way we looked at home computers by making them cheaper and more accessible. Steve Jobs and Steve Wozniak were the disruptive innovators behind that shift in perception. More recently, Evan Spiegel and Bobby Murphy, knowing that people were getting paranoid about the permanence of photos being uploaded to the internet (primarily Facebook), came up with the 'self-destruct' smartphone app, Snapchat. It allows users to share an image or video and then literally have it disappear seconds later, after it's viewed. On a daily basis, at its height, Snapchat users were sharing 100 million images daily. This is innovation and disruption without aggression and with collaboration.

Similarly, Jennifer Hyman and Jenny Fleiss of Rent the Runway have redefined the way ordinary women are able to enjoy exclusive designer dresses. The opportunity to wear designer special-occasion frocks is simply not available to the majority of the population, so they either settle for an inexpensive imitation or purchase something expensive, wear it and then return it. Rent the Runway purchases these dresses and hires them out on a nightly basis, meaning customers are able to enjoy the experience of amazing garments without the hefty price tag. 'Our intention is to disrupt every part of what retail has meant historically,' Hyman has said. They have proven so successful they are backed by US$55.4 million in funding and employ 200 people, including a large dry-cleaning service.

These two recent examples of disruptive innovators show that it is not necessary to be cut-throat and ruthless in order to disrupt. It is about looking outside the boundaries to innovation and a different way — and it is absolutely about collaboration and partnership. It is also clearly about listening to the customer and giving them what they want, which is a collaborative way of working in itself — and in some ways it is disruptive, because within a traditional business model and a Me way of thinking, the customer's thoughts and feelings are not always considered.

To be a disrupter can sometimes mean facing ridicule and failure. It means having enough self-confidence and self-belief to be proactive rather than reactive in the face of naysayers. This can be irrespective of sector, profile or generation and gender.

Food for disruptive thought

In *The Innovator's DNA*, Jeff Dyer, Hal Gregersen and the previously mentioned Clayton M. Christensen discuss the characteristics that make up leaders who are capable of this kind of behaviour and how they apply in practice to innovative entrepreneurs.

There are five skills that disruptive leaders possess:

1 associating

2 questioning

3 observing

4 networking

5 experimenting.

The first is a thinking skill and the latter four are behavioural. The key point of their discussion is essential to the We space: in order to act differently, one has to think differently. And to be in the We space, you must be prepared to think on a different level — and again it comes back to disruption.

The great thing for any leader willing to work towards the We space is that these aren't necessarily inbuilt traits, but learned ones. As mentioned in ReConnect Principle 2 — Build a diverse network, networking is a skill that you can work on, and in fact works best when you are being assisted by others (this forms the kernel of a successful network — goodwill). Also part of the collaborative process is experimentation — which goes hand in hand with a willingness to fail, another trait of the disrupter.

Being able to enjoy the element of surprise within a business setting and integrate it into planning is also key to the makeup of a successful disruptive leader. Many leaders assume surprise should always be avoided. This isn't the case. Surprise can certainly be inherently risky. Failures, successes, unexpected technological advancements, competitive moves, customer feedback, political and regulatory shifts: all of these have an element of surprise to them but, for a disrupter, they can also be turned to the positive and used as a strategic tool, especially if they think collaboratively, because a team approach will ensure there is a range of the best ideas available to cope with the uncertain.

Disruption takes many forms. Whether it is questioning the status quo, forming a more effective network or changing procedures, all disrupters have one thing in common — the wish to see change happen.

Case study—disruption creates a new movement

Renata Cooper is the founder of Forming Circles, the unique Australian organisation that is committed to providing opportunities for Australian individuals and groups in areas of small business, education, arts, innovation and charitable projects. Founded at the end of 2011, it was incorporated as an ethical and social investment company.

Renata came to Australia from her native Slovakia as a teenager. Speaking no English, with no money and no support, she set herself the goal of educating herself and was determined to give back to her new country. In addition to Forming Circles, she is now part of an 'angel investor' group that concentrates on financial independence for female entrepreneurs. She is a frequent commentator on financial matters in the Australian and international media.

In terms of what they are doing to help put collaborative methods into practice, entrepreneurs such as Renata Cooper are the early adopters of the We way of leading. The mindset, ethics and values that they show are those of the brave, the disruptive and those who are willing to lead by example. Leadership such as this is to be encouraged—but there are those who still see witchcraft in the wisdom and the ability to be forward-thinking.

Renata shares her thoughts:

> There is an immense value in commercial collaboration as a way of doing business. The key driver of commercial collaboration is the mutually beneficial ROI achieved by collaborating. To that end, there is significant value in people or entities working together to achieve common goals.

> In a decentralised, digital and collaborative economy and environment, we will see an increase in commercial collaboration as people try to maintain lean operations

while providing more business solutions. Collaboration also has the benefit of scaling up talent and value propositions to suit customer requirements.

As cited by *TIME* magazine in 2011, collaborative consumption is one of the '10 ideas that will change the world'. Since 2011, we've seen a dramatic shift in businesses adopting a more agile model suited to the rapidly changing economy.

Just as commercial collaboration is on the rise as a business methodology, so too are female entrepreneurs working within this model. They are truly starting to shape business practices within Australia by working collaboratively, and the situation is similar in first-world countries overseas, especially the US. Working collaboratively is one of the best things for female entrepreneurs — especially time-poor women juggling families.

Digital technologies have brought the world closer and shrunk marketplaces. This has given more women the courage to take on new business challenges, safe with the knowledge that they can collaborate to bring in the right team, resources, funding, creativity and mentorship to achieve ROI and succeed. Women entrepreneurs will be the early adopters leading this change for the rest of the market.

Just as commercial collaboration is becoming of prime importance, so too are individual business principles, which are shaped from one's own journey. My business journey started with the realisation I wanted to step away from a background in financial markets to start something that would make a difference to the world around me. I wanted to create a business model that would fulfil this objective and also be sustainable.

When I started networking with women in business, I realised two things: there was a need for more awareness about education and there were many women with great ideas who weren't being mentored, supported or getting adequate funding to execute their business ideas or growth to the next level.

This led to the inception of Forming Circles in 2011. The business model is founded using tools of the 21st century, such as social media, crowd-funding campaigns and innovative thinking, and the more traditional method of driving positive word-of-mouth through effective actions. Collaboration was a big part of the disruptive model I adopted. For example, I collaborated with other leading women entrepreneurs who came on board as mentors in their respective fields for the Kickstart Your Business Grant that we offer. It allows me to offer a more comprehensive solution to the winners of the grant.

Success comes from being a visionary in the space you are operating in. This can be as simple as approaching a problem a different way or by creating innovative products and services. Look at the world around you and push the boundaries. Women often hold back as there isn't a 'tried and tested pathway' for what they want to achieve. Be disruptive by starting the trend and set the agenda for others to follow.

The other key principle I follow is to see the vision and work backwards from there. For me, the vision was growth through positive investments with impact. I then deconstructed not only how I would do this, but also how to do it well. Some people get so caught up in the tasks that they lose sight of the vision.

A key area of importance for commercial collaboration is how females work to support each other in this space, particularly female leaders. There is such a need for sponsorship—active sponsorship—within the business and entrepreneurial arena, for women, by women. The prevalence of supporting other women in business has definitely picked up in recent years as more entrepreneurs entered the market, and also with global acknowledgement of the importance of women entrepreneurs to the economic structures of countries. From an investing point of view, I can say that there is room for more women to become involved as angel investors.

The angel investment market is not as mature as in the US, so it has been slower taking off in Australia. The involvement of entities such as Scale Investors, myself and other women investing in another's business will hopefully inspire more women to get involved.

Many corporates, especially banks, have divisions set up to mentor and support women in business. For example, Commonwealth Bank has the Women in Focus platform and NAB has their Women in Leadership Awards. Corporate Australia is recognising the powerful force that female entrepreneurs are, and is increasing its support in the community to see it grow. Likewise, there are other groups such as the AWCCI and Springboard Enterprises providing invaluable mentorship and guidance to support women entrepreneurs.

It's wonderful to see the rise of support for female entrepreneurs, and I feel it is down to this new collaborative environment of female-centric angel investors. They have a definitively different approach from male-led teams, but this space allows for that, and it only adds value. Female-centric angel investors started in recognition of women's hesitancy in asking for finance and/or funding and their comfort in working with other women. The GEDI (Global Entrepreneurship Development Institute) report noted that for every 100 businesses started by men in Australia, 85 were started by women, and the fact that only 5 per cent of women received venture capital illustrates the lack of support for this growing segment of the economy.

Admittedly, acting collaboratively is still a relatively new way of doing business for large corporates. For generations, we've seen brands built on IP, core value, good leadership and great content. Now, in a connected digital world, a lot of those frameworks are a thing of the past. Users create IP and content, and leadership is defined not by the ability to lead, but how well you engage.

Disruptive practices have become the new normal and many corporates with a history of hierarchy will have to undergo significant change management to come to terms with this.

Case study—an intrepid disrupter

There are those who sit within the public services of their countries, quietly serving out their time, without public recognition, without fanfare, without any kind of glory. Then there are those who decide not necessarily that they need the trumpets to sound, but more that they need to shake up the system. One of those people is Chris Allen.

Chris began his career as a soldier and was commissioned as an officer. He served with the Royal Australian Regiment, qualified as a paratrooper in Australia, the UK and France, undertook attachments to the Officer Cadet School of New Zealand and the British Parachute Regiment and deployed to South-East Asia, Africa and Central America.

After leaving the military due to extensive injuries, he was engaged in humanitarian aid work for CARE International during the 1999 East Timor emergency and in the wake of September 11, 2001 became involved in Australian government protective security. Chris provided top-level advice to commonwealth agencies and diplomatic residences as a member of the Australian Federal Police Protective Service, and led the Counter Terrorist First Response Force at Sydney Airport in 2002.

After being headhunted to oversee an unprecedented security upgrade of Australia's iconic landmark, the Sydney Opera House, he later held the position of Sheriff of New South Wales, one of Australia's most historic appointments, from 2008 until 2012.

At no time in his career has he settled for safety. He has always taken the road less travelled, both through lateral transfers to another Commonwealth country's defence force and through working in several war zones, both within the armed forces and as a civilian. That he then took on the role of Sheriff of New South Wales, and then self-published as an author, sums up a career of disruption and innovation.

Chris's first novel in the Intrepid series, *Defender*, was self-published before being re-released by Momentum Books with his second novel, *Hunter*, at the end of 2012. Both novels rocketed to the top of the charts on iTunes and Amazon, with *Hunter* becoming a bestseller. There is currently a US film/TV franchise in development based on his novels. His third title in the series, *Avenger*, will be published next year.

For someone to leave the security of the Australian Public Service and strike out into the volatile world of authorship — and self-published authorship at that — takes a great deal of self-belief. It also means facing the two big 'no-no's' of leadership: one's own fear and vulnerabilities.

It could be said that as an ex-paratrooper with the elite Paras of 16 Air Assault Brigade (formerly 5 Paras), the fears had already well and truly been faced, but these were different fears: the fears of taking on responsibility for planning out an entire business — not only writing a book, but seeing it through the process of publishing, the publicity campaign, the social media push, promotion and liaising with distributors, the fan base and reviewers. In other words, juggling several balls and keeping all of said balls happy.

Unfortunately, there was not the option to quietly shoot any of them if they became unhappy — it really didn't fit the business model. For Chris, his background in the military establishment and working in the incredibly complex world of international aid agencies assisted him in his current career, and in taking a collaborative approach:

> One of the biggest things I learned to an extent in the military, but mostly in post-military life, is that there are so many different agendas and people you need to engage with, that you can't just blindly belt your way through—you have to be accommodating of other people's beliefs and agendas; it can't be all about 'what's in it for me professionally'. You have to consider instead what do *they* need professionally—and be open and honest and transparent about your objectives.

He has had a lot of frustrations with publishers and agents, but contends that you can't take the old-school straightforward military way. You must be aware of all factors at play—there are always things beneath the surface. For him, collaboration is about embracing the needs of the other people you are working with—and to make sure you are giving back as well.

His involvement in international humanitarian aid work was the first environment in which this was seen immediately on a large scale; there were so many stakeholders involved, with so many different agendas to push: the UN, the local and international military, local communities, East Timorese. It was a Canadian a few years older than Chris—for whom aid work was a true vocation, and for whom dealing with a million different stakeholders at once was seen as routine—who helped Chris get the attitude right with the UN.

> It comes down to what you want—and that's to keep thinking bigger. Keep your eye always on the mission objective. Think in military terms—it may sound clichéd, but the best-laid plans never survive the first shot, so you just have to change plans and keep going. There will always, always be naysayers—ignore them, focus on those who want to collaborate and be positive—and know that success is always the end goal. Understand your own vision, and keep true to what that vision is, and again, ignore the obstacles and people with other agendas. If people are not in the same space as you—you have got to let them go. Not everyone is interested in what collaborative thinking has to offer.

Chris has never settled for the status quo and what could be termed 'easy' success. At the same time, he has always seen the value in the collaborative space. For someone bred in the competitive 'alpha' environment of the armed forces, it just goes to show the power of the disruptive mind and the impact it has on those around it.

Checklist — ReConnect Principle 4: Disrupt

Holding the status quo means repeating the ordinary over and over; suppressing the stronger impulses and the extraordinary ideas. Disrupting the typical business model means enabling change — which means enabling collaboration and leading-edge methods. It means including others in what you are doing. It means decisiveness. It's challenging and confronting.

It's future-proofing your success.

☑ Are you willing to collaborate and change?

☑ Are you willing to think with agility?

☑ Are you ready to involve others in what you want to achieve?

☑ Do you want to see the everyday become the extraordinary?

☑ Do you see your business as extending outside the boardroom?

☑ Do you thrive on challenges?

☑ Are you ready to empower others?

☑ Do you have an active network?

☑ Do you question decisions?

☑ Do you associate ideas, people and thoughts?

chapter 10

ReConnect Principle 5— Exchange value

Price is what you pay, value is what you get.

— Warren Buffett, investor and philanthropist

Commercial collaboration requires a value exchange in the true sense of the term, in that it requires both parties to bring something more to the transaction than just a product at a price.

At its heart, a value exchange is a very simple process; it is, by literal definition, a transfer of goods or services from a company to its customers, with the customer paying for the goods or services in return. The 'but wait, there's more' comes in because 'value' lies in the need the good or service fulfils, rather than its actual physical properties.

When you look at it like that, it's not very complicated. But when you take in the intrinsic worth of the value *add,* and what a value exchange stands for when it comes to commercial collaboration — then lines begin to blur.

We all use the term and nod sagely whenever anyone introduces the concept into conversation — 'the long-term benefits of the inherent value exchange between X and Y can't be underestimated' — but just how *much* value (pardon the pun) does it actually add to everyday business relationships and future success?

A value exchange gives both parties the chance to bring something more to the transaction than just a product. Say you are selling a pair of shoes. The value exchange is not just about the leather and rubber used to manufacture the product in exchange for a price; it's about:

- the media campaign designed to catch the eye of the consumer when they are flicking through a magazine

- making the consumer know that they will look and feel better if they have *that* particular pair of shoes on their feet

- follow-up customer service when that particular pair of shoes has been ordered online, to see if the consumer is happy with their purchase.

That is a value exchange. The consumer receives something *more* than just a product and, in return, the business receives inestimable goodwill — and future sales.

The value of exchange

A perfect example of business-to-consumer value exchange is the Michelin Guides. First published in 1900, they began as very simple handbooks with handy information about where to stop for food, accommodation and petrol. (Not many places in 1900!) Now they have evolved into the most prestigious restaurant rating system in the world, with only 86 three-star Michelin-rated restaurants across the planet. To use the Michelin Guides is a completely interactive experience, with the customers themselves involved in the process of selecting who's hot and who's not. They are a part of the experience, and thus not only gain information, but added value.

Modern brands do the same thing — and also from business to business. Mailchimp sends you tutorials after you sign up, whether you use their free service or their premium. This is a great example of true collaborative commercialism — and yes, there is marketing sense behind it, because the more you know about Mailchimp and how good it is, the more likely you are to use the premium service.

To be cynical about this — and it is something that one has to bear in mind when it comes to collaborative business practices — content only delivers engagement if it confers value over and above simply promoting the brand that generates it. If it can't do that, it's nothing more than an advertisement. Collaboration — or the purest principle of the value exchange — equals talking *with*, not talking at.

In the same way, working collaboratively with other entrepreneurs, or corporate leaders, can be its own form of value exchange with immeasurable market potential, as long as all parties are willing to be open in their engagement. If they are empty in their approach, or withhold ideas, information or best business practices, then there is no true value exchange — rather an empty shell of potential.

Person X, or even Company X, may have expertise in a certain area, but be falling down badly in another. They know that Person Y or Company Y has the skills and knowledge base they need for a successful new product launch, or company growth — and is not in any way in competition with them — but X has been too inward-looking and wary to admit they need help, or fear being judged as weak. If they think of opening up to Y as a value exchange, offering their own skill sets and contacts in another area as an attraction, rather than seeing their 'lack' as a weakness, the potential for collaborative business, and growth for both businesses, is enormous — commercially and emotionally.

Value exchange is the free giving and exchanging of ideas, knowledge and insight with no expectation of anything in return. Some may refer to it as 'what goes around comes around'. Others refer to the Law of Reciprocity, a social convention where we feel the need to repay in kind that which another has provided.

Irrespective of your view, the active exchange of value is a must in the new We economy and this takes trust, faith and the ability to turn outward rather than always facing in — trusting others rather than just yourself. The benefits of adopting Principle 5, Exchange value, are enormous. The value exchange is not just financial; it's emotional too. You invest emotionally in your customers' happiness every time you make sure that they receive the very best product you are able to produce. You are willing to give your customers 100 per cent, so why shouldn't you give your business that same amount of energy and attention? You invest in your business relationships and your diverse and powerful network, through frank and open exchange of intelligence, by opening up business opportunities or by sponsoring an introduction between two parties, knowing that opportunity lies within that connection.

Louise Agnew, founder and principal of Lyfe Academy, states:

> Collaboration is about opening up to new possibilities in life by listening, learning and growing, by sharing with inspiring people who lift you higher and help change your perspectives through sharing.

Ultimately everyone has to bring something to the table — you have to be able to deliver and do what you say you are going to do. We all want the best; we all strive to attain. It is human nature to want more. The magic of commercial collaboration and the value exchange in the We economy is that their impact affects multiple dimensions across all areas of business.

The value exchange vs the fear of imitation

Imitation is said to be the greatest form of flattery, yet when it happens many of us find it a bitter pill to swallow. In the collaborative economy, how do you manage the risk of copycat behaviour against the benefits of sharing business insight and IP?

We have all been there at some stage of our business lives, whether it is with an idea or a product. One day we're the only one in town with this 'unique selling point'; the next, there are three people at our heels with a concept that feels horribly familiar. 'That's okay,' we say to ourselves comfortably, 'there's always room in the market for competition — and besides, the original is always the best, right?'

But what happens when business becomes personal, and what we have perceived as flattery — someone we trust showing an interest and excitement about what we do — turns into imitation? How are we supposed to feel when an open and collaborative approach to business backfires, and suddenly a protégé becomes a rival for market share?

This can be one of the hardest situations you can possibly face within the commercial collaboration space. When you are determining the direction of your business on a daily basis and working innovatively, bringing new ideas to your industry and sphere of operations, to watch as someone seems to piggyback from your work and talent can be devastating, if you allow it to be.

This is the key: if *you allow* it to be.

In whatever you do, there is always going to be a limited amount of time where you are the only player in the market. If you have a great idea, it is inevitable that others are going to see its inherent value, and either (in the worst scenario) directly copy it, or in some cases, improve on it. What happens to your business will be directly dependent on your attitude to those who follow in your footsteps.

If you believe in working openly and honestly and, yes, collaboratively, your intellectual property is going to be available to others. What is integral to you staying true to yourself is your ability to cope when someone chooses to (and I do put this term in quotation marks for a reason), 'abuse' their knowledge of your vision. You have a product; they use what they have learned from you to make product Mk II. Whether it is a success or not is dependent on how they execute their idea, but do not forget that the reason the Mk II has appeared is because your product is a success.

After having a quiet scream, my advice to you is this:

- Do see it as flattery; if you weren't doing something amazing, they wouldn't be trying to do it too.

- Make sure that your core business ideas are protected — the onus is on you to insure your intellectual property.

- Remember that business is business, and lines will be crossed; sometimes the personal will be blurred — it isn't nice, but it is human nature.

- Be restless to stay ahead of the game — at all times have a number of 'new ideas' bubbling and in development.

- Don't retreat into secret squirrel mode, but rather think long and hard about what you can do better, and ask for feedback from your closest supporters.

- Find your voice, and stand even more in your own spotlight.

Case study — exchanging value drives business expansion

Suzie Hoitink is a prime example of how truly successful commercial collaboration can be — both to her, and to the people she is connected to. Suzie, the founder and CEO of Clear Complexions clinics, is a Telstra Award–winning businesswoman who knew the value of what she was doing within her own home state, but also realised that she was limited geographically. As a result, she joined a women's networking group and, through the connections she made there, was able to not only see a way forward to expand her business into other states, but also how to strategically position herself in terms of launching that new endeavour and marketing value-adds to the business.

Suzie has also been able to raise the profile of the women she networks with through cross-promotion in her new publication featuring their stories. Her drive, determination and above all her honest and transparent approach to working collaboratively, making it clear what she is able to offer, has helped her to add value to her connections as they add value to her.

They say that what doesn't kill you makes you stronger. In the case of Suzie Hoitink, it made her an award-winning owner of her own business, across two states and four locations, with unique positioning and thought leadership status within her industry.

All within seven years.

They also say 'work with what you know'. In Suzie's case, this was her own experience with bad skin. In her teens, she suffered badly from heavy acne, pigmentation and scarring. It affected her physical and mental attitude to life; she became withdrawn, used heavy makeup and suffered badly from depression. All of these things added to her determination and drive just a few years later, when, after graduating with her nursing degree, she began working for a cosmetic surgeon who was 'dabbling' with light-based therapies as a way of treating scarring from acne, rosacea and pigmentation. She tasked herself with finding out more, and rapidly realised that it was an untapped opportunity.

Who better than a qualified nurse to both:

- understand the ramifications of the treatment on a clinical level

- truly give the patients the reassurance and proper follow-up care they needed?

In 2005, the first Clear Complexions clinic opened in Canberra. It was an immediate success. Suzie made it mandatory for only doctors or nurses to treat patients. She introduced cutting-edge technology, and the follow-up program for patients was second to none. Expansion within the ACT was rapid, and Suzie's approach to networking within the territory—and within her industry—was exemplary. When she realised she was limited by her lack of networks outside the ACT, and that her ambition and drive meant expansion outside of the ACT was needed, she acknowledged that in order to successfully achieve her dreams she needed to seek out diverse connections that would challenge her thinking, add value to her plans and open doors that were previously closed.

She knew her area of expertise and was confident in that area of her business; she had the staff to support her in the expansion of her business. But she felt that many traditional networking groups were not going to give her the level of support and forward thinking she needed to take her business to the next level:

> I find 'traditional' networking methods don't tend to add a lot of value to my business, nor are they really all that enjoyable ... I find that I get so much more done, and feel like I am making truly valuable connections, when I am in an environment which is much more intimate. [A] recent limited numbers seminar that [was] held, where everyone had a chance to be truly involved and participate and find out relevant answers from great businesspeople — that's what networking should be about.

Suzie joined LBDGroup, which is known for its non-traditional approach to networking. Through LBDGroup, she was connected to a diverse group of female entrepreneurs and thought leaders. The conversations that she engaged in contributed to the business-plan development for her NSW launch, in particular with regard to the clinic's opening model and its appropriateness for the NSW market.

Suzie's confidence in her vision and direction grew. This inner confidence enabled her to be risk tolerant of the conversation, challenges and contributions being made. She was courageous enough to disrupt her existing and proven successful launch-to-market model for clinics in the ACT, to develop a new approach, more suited to the NSW market where her brand was unknown.

Suzie quickly engaged the cream of the crop in terms of PR, social media and marketing expertise to enable her launch — all through active sponsoring and introductions.

March 2013 saw the first interstate Clear Complexions clinic open in the Sydney suburb of Balmain. This was a huge move for an established market leader known only to customers in the ACT. The lack of brand awareness wasn't the only challenge—the Sydney market is highly competitive.

But, as Suzie says, 'We had prepared for years by perfecting our systems, education processes and procedure manuals to ensure there was consistency of care across all clinics'.

The first clinic opened with minimal marketing dollars but with the significant presence and support of LBDGroup members, affiliation marketing at no cost to Suzie and the leveraging of networks to deliver media exposure, influencer programs, a well-attended launch event, speaking engagements and client referrals.

Suzie embodies the ideals of working collaboratively through understanding the 'value' of value exchange. She has actively gained business and profile from the support of her network, but at the same time she has given back by giving others exposure in her new publication. LBDGroup members are invited to contribute to the free-to-subscribers magazine, which gives Suzie content, but also gives the contributors key placement and marketing opportunities, which they then cross-promote on their own social media channels.

This is Me to We in practice. A smaller business recognising the value of a larger network, and the larger network responding to transparent business methods and honesty of purpose and ambition. As Suzie says:

I never had a mentor when starting Clear Complexions although I often wished I did. Back then I relied on instinct. Now I surround myself with talented and successful businesswomen through networking groups like Women in Focus and LBDGroup. Through the Telstra Awards I have also forged strong relationships with focused and generous women who are always there when I need the 'push' or the 'pull back'.

I have learnt two things from these women; firstly reciprocity, to share knowledge freely and expect nothing in return; and secondly to stand out—be brave and bold.

One of the key things Suzie attributes to her success is the people she collaborates actively with:

> Surround yourself with like-minded people who will support and inspire you, share what you know and your experiences and give back to your community. In fact, give back 'til it hurts.

Relationships are all there is. Everything in the universe only exists because it is in relationship to everything else. Nothing exists in isolation. We have to stop pretending we are individuals that can go it alone.

— Margaret J. Wheatley, author of *Turning To One Another*

Case study—A stylish exchange

Some industries are renowned for their 'closed door' approach to outsiders. Nobody is allowed in, and woe betide those who attempt entry without the secret knock or code word. But for two women with an incredible amount of determination and drive, the real estate sector in Melbourne has opened up to purely because they have proven themselves—and because they have shown that they have something to offer the industry other than just a banner advertisement in the Saturday papers.

Sara and Amy Chamberlain came from incredibly disparate backgrounds to fulfil a long-held dream to start a successful business together. They have done this admirably, and in an incredibly short time frame. After starting The Real Estate Stylist in early 2012, they came to public attention when Rebecca Judd, wife of AFL high-flyer Chris Judd, praised the work they did on the property she was selling in Melbourne.

Suddenly, The Real Estate Stylist was a hot (excuse the pun) property.

The Chamberlains are a perfect example of finding a niche market and excelling in it. They have taken a dream, envisioned it and realised it. They are showing true bravery in business, and also the collaborative spirit in their relationships with real estate agents.

The recipe for success is simple in theory:

- Find a unique selling point.
- Add determination, drive and incredible marketing skills.
- Throw in a good network of contacts.
- Find a client who is willing to take a chance—and then actively promote you.
- Become a viable business.

Ninety-five per cent of new businesses fail because one of these ingredients simply doesn't gel. The drive is there, but the product doesn't catch the market's eye. Contacts don't quite live up to their promises of actively promoting and engaging their networks. The clients—well, they don't materialise.

For the very, very determined 5 per cent, however, welcome to the world of The Real Estate Stylist.

Sara and Amy Chamberlain had no experience of the real estate market beyond having invested on a personal level themselves, when in early 2012 they made the decision to (finally) go into business together.

They have incredibly diverse backgrounds; Amy was a primary school teacher, Sara an advertising and marketing guru. What they had was a recognition that in a straitened economic climate, those seeking to sell their properties for the best possible price—or, in fact, to attract a buyer at all—needed an edge.

And that edge was to have their property presented as well as possible—which meant professional styling. Nobody was really doing it in Melbourne, or at least not at the level the two women proposed: with the sellers having vacated the property and the entire place emptied of their furniture, lock, stock and barrel. This was not a 'makeover'; it was a complete restyle. And it was not going to be cheap.

Both women are intensively creative and forward thinking, and with Sara having the marketing background to drive a business plan, they understood the fundamentals of a new enterprise in a niche market that was yet to be explored. This was not just about running a business; this was about something far bigger and more disruptive.

Sara expanded on this point:

> It's very alluring to say 'I am currently working for someone else at X rate for five days a week; why don't I do it for myself at Y rate for three days a week?'—but if you are going into business with that mindset, you are choosing a lifestyle rather than aiming for the stars. Be prepared to turn your life upside down for five years, know in your gut what you want and don't tell too many people to start with. There are always naysayers who will try to drag you down. Conversely, I firmly believe in the maxim 'don't let flattery be your business strategy'. People may encourage us to do a lot of different things, because they feel we have the talents or capability for them—but if it doesn't fit your base business model, keep the training wheels on.

Neither sister gives less than 100 per cent to the business. They both have long-term plans for its success that they will act on by being rational and thoughtful—but also by thinking laterally and with imagination.

The sisters also acknowledged that their vision would be realised through relationships—not just with clients, although as it turned out, it was an early client who really brought them to public attention—but through an incredibly powerful industry sector: real estate agents.

Recommendations from agents would be invaluable to The Real Estate Stylist's business, and this collaborative commercial relationship would have its own value for the agents. Obviously, if a property sold because of the way it was presented, the chances of repeat business were going to grow. Agents would recommend the sisters to new sellers—and it becomes symbiotic. This is what value exchange is all about.

It was a form of collaboration unfamiliar to the real estate sector, and it was something that the women wanted to encourage. They agreed that the best experience and the best result for the client comes when there is a close relationship with the agent, and when it is collaborative and a united front is presented for the vendors. They are a service provider, and the agent is better served by giving the best service provider possible to add value to the vendor. It becomes about the team, especially if the agent is open in saying, 'I don't have the expertise in this area, but these people do'. It's professional and tightens the brand, as well as providing a working relationship, which is not only mutually beneficial, but also mutually satisfying.

This is not only commercial collaboration, but also value exchange at work, and having open and transparent business relationships. There are challenges for them, as there are of course now imitators within the marketplace. This is where attitude—that of bravery versus bravado—wins out.

Case study—a luxurious alliance

It takes great skill to hide the fact that you have great skill.

— Francois de La Rochefoucauld, writer

When it was founded in 1954, the Comité Colbert was seen almost as an exclusive 'boys' club' of luxury manufacturers. Now, it is one of the most important international examples of the way collaborative business principles—and in particular value exchange—work in practice.

The creation of Jean-Jacques Guerlain, the Comité Colbert is named after the man made minister of finance by Louis XIV in 1661. This visionary Frenchman saw that the mercantile future of France lay with the fruits of its exquisite culture. Colbert used his financial acumen and his epicurean taste as a renowned art collector to promote export trade (forming the East and West Indies Trading Company) and in so doing made French craftsmanship known across the globe.

The Comité began with 14 'maisons', or houses, from the French haute couture sector. With names such as Chanel, Hermès, Krug, Le Meurice and the Hotel Plaza Athénée among its French maisons, in its present inception it has expanded to cover eight sectors and has 75 members, representing not only France, but also the European Union—including Hungary (Herend), The Czech Republic (Moser), Poland (Dr Irena Eris) and Germany (Montblanc and Leica). To become a member, each maison must meet and conform to five incredibly strict criteria:

- international ambition and a unique character
- quality
- design
- ethics
- a concentration on the 'poetry of the object'.

The founding members of the Comité Colbert were quick to realise that the luxury goods market was rapidly reaching a point where there was no growth, and the appeal of its goods were waning. The answer lay in a collaborative approach to the way the maisons worked. Only through sharing knowledge, business practices, contacts, export partnerships—only through truly transparent relationships and a commitment to celebrating quality could they achieve what, ultimately, every business had to keep as the forefront of their thought process: a healthy bottom line.

LVMH (in its various individual brands) is an integral part of the Comité Colbert—in many ways, it embodies in one corporation the principles the Comité has instigated. As Bernard Arnault, CEO of LVMH, says:

> …we are really very lucky to have so many fantastic brands. But to grow them we should not be too much in a hurry. They are growing fast, but they have to grow accordingly to the market and to the capacity we have to deliver good products.

Herein lies the philosophy, in practice, of the Comité Colbert; a concentration on ambition but with an understanding that design and quality are essential to the standing of the product. To achieve this, they are willing to work in collaboration with other bodies to keep standards incredibly high.

Said Elisabeth Ponsolle des Portes, president and CEO of the Comité, at the time of a highly successful anti-counterfeiting campaign:

> The protection of intellectual property rights makes it possible to grow competitive French businesses and safeguard French jobs. The combat of the Comité Colbert, which is of long date, illustrates the luxury sector's commitment to the fight against counterfeiting to protect our know-how and creation.

Herein lies the inherent need for a true value exchange within the Comité's various houses and also within the French and EU economies. There has to be an absolutely open sharing of knowledge, facts and to some extent skills and intellectual property in terms of counterfeiting methods, for example, between similar design houses. In this way standards can be upheld across the entire sector instead of being uneven from country to country. This is one of the benefits of having the Comité extend beyond French borders; it means self-interest from the entire EU and also collaboration across the region on what is acceptable in the luxury sector. In the days of the Cold War, shoddy copies would have been made behind the Iron Curtain. Now, the Czech Republic and Poland are members. They have a vested interest in the value exchange being even.

We all want the best; we all strive to attain. It is human nature. The Comité Colbert has been shrewd enough to see the inherent value in pursuing this, and at the same time preserving the best of European — and in particular, French — culture. This is collaborative thinking for financial, historical and ethical goals.

Who can argue with that?

Checklist — ReConnect Principle 5: Exchange value

You are bringing something of yourself, your company and your leadership to a transaction. You are willing to exchange knowledge or add value in order to show good faith and start a collaborative relationship. This is about goodwill and future-proofing success — not just for you, but also for another business, for your customers, for their customers, for your team, for your colleagues.

What needs to be considered to make this value exchange viable, relevant and worthwhile?

☑ Do you have expertise that is needed by another entity?

☑ Are you willing to share it openly?

☑ Are you looking for anything in return?

☑ What are you doing to protect your intellectual property?

☑ What is this relationship's value-add to your business?

☑ Are you willing to accept being seen as vulnerable if you ask for help?

☑ Are you willing to not withhold ideas and information?

chapter 11

ReConnect Principle 6 — Think bigger

> If you think big, then it's going to be big.
>
> — *Emeril Lagasse, celebrity chef*

Pursue your goals with relentless determination, think bigger, get out of your own way and walk determinedly on the road to success.

In 1970, a young man decided to capitalise on his love of listening to music by selling records to other kids who wanted a fun place to hang out while they chose what music to buy.

In 2014, that young (at heart) man had a worldwide group of companies that numbered around four hundred, employed more than 50 000 people and has a net worth of $US5 billion. He is the CEO of — yes, you guessed it — the Virgin Group.

This is aiming for the stars. And part of Richard Branson's phenomenal success is not only his ability to think bigger, but to base that big thinking on a principle that is lacking in a lot of traditional business leaders.

It's the art of making a decision, because:

Decision + Action = Change

And change is at the foundation of truly big thinking. Branson recognises that without the ability to make (and take) decisions, that *sine qua non* of good leadership, the could-be-goods are rapidly separated from the greats. For example, each Virgin business is an autonomous body, with strong management teams having a say in every decision. Good ideas are rapidly encouraged and promoted. Risks are taken. If they fail, they fail, but a decision is made all the same. And, in turn, the button is pushed on 80 per cent of launches.

Like several other highly successful entrepreneurs and game changers, Branson sees the success in 'launch, learn, evolve'.

Think about the most successful entrepreneurs of the past 50 years. Steve Jobs. Edwin Land. Mark Zuckerberg. Larry Page and Sergey Brin. Jim Sinegal. Bill Gates.

They all had a dream. They all continued, or continue, to dream. They all, in one way or another, took a risk in order to live by those dreams. Think of Steve Jobs leaving the security of Apple when he wasn't happy with its direction — and founding Pixar.

Things are changing incredibly rapidly; the business cycle is significantly shorter. New competitors are emerging every day, and the interconnectivity of the global economy and speed of technology mean change is ever present and phenomenally fast. You have what you know is a brilliant idea; you take your time mulling over the various outcomes for it — and then someone else goes to market or shares the same idea at a meeting, and the opportunity is lost. It's all very well to say 'that was my idea' — but if you haven't made a decision on what to do with it, where's the value?

The plethora of choices in terms of how to launch — whether it be a product, a new professional standard or intellectual property — seems to be bogging down the process of actually getting from the 'Eureka' moment to market. With so many options in terms of suppliers, design and launch mechanisms, it seems we are unable to actually make a decision. So how do we overcome the need to have an idea at the 100 per cent–right point before we are willing to say 'just do it'?

Game changers vs game resisters

Leaders in business today need to hone their decision-making skills in order to make game-changing leaps. This leadership skill is becoming most needed. You must set a big-picture vision with goals to get there and then make a decision on:

- what to deliver

- how to deliver

- how to measure

- how to decide to continue or move on if a decision doesn't pay off (believe me they sometimes won't).

If you continually search for perfection, then inevitably someone else will take the golden ring. Focus on getting it 100 per cent right and you will find yourself well and truly frozen and, at times, may feel like everyone and everything is moving at warp speed around you. Focus on the 'to do list' rather than the launch, and the moment has gone with you slapping yourself for thinking great things, but not acting on them.

There are so many negatives that can impede us from thinking big in business, and it can be incredibly hard to overcome them, especially when trying to launch a new idea, product or model. The Game Resisters overthink the process: 'What if I mess this up? What if I lose my business? My job? What if I trust the wrong experts? What if I am letting too much knowledge out?'

Fear is not your friend

It's incredibly easy to let fear overtake us — and that's exactly what overthinking amounts to. Fear. So embrace that fear and turn it around. Yes, you may mess it up. But equally imagine all you will learn in the process. You may more likely succeed. If you don't try, it will be a permanent Schrödinger's Cat — a paradox.

We all procrastinate, putting off that which scares us, or seems too hard. The only thing that should belong in our minds is self-belief, innovation and dreams. Face your fears.

The limitations and barriers that we put in our way, if we allow them to, do the following:

- become self-sabotaging
- block creative time
- drain our energy.

These are things we do to create failure before we even have a chance to succeed, to think big. 'We should have. We could have. We would have. We can't' are all part of the game resister palette.

But if we truly want to be the next Steve Jobs, the next Mark Zuckerberg, the next Sara Blakely; if we want to change our own game, business or industry, we have to do the following:

- step up to the plate
- face the fear
- focus
- believe
- have vision and courage
- engage in active teamwork
- keep eyes, ears and minds open for opportunity
- strive for continual innovation and perfection.

Find a way to achieve the big-picture goal by:

- using the power of technology and mass communication to reach further than ever before possible
- being so focused on the end game that every decision is a step in that same direction
- harnessing and powering up the collaborative talent of those individuals you trust
- making the most of relationships in a business sense which are open, transparent and mutually beneficial

- building a dream team around you
- creating a culture that:
  - enables freedom to explore
  - has an inbuilt curiosity to develop and test
  - sees opportunity and learning in mistakes and failures
  - believes in success: that we can, we will and we are.

Fail your way to success

Sara Blakely is a perfect example of thinking big — and then thinking bigger and biggest. At 29, she invested her $5000 life savings in finding something to flatter her figure under her white slacks. Six months later, the one-time Disney World ride greeter and door-to-door fax machine salesperson found her new line of shaping underwear, Spanx, named one of Oprah's 'Favourite Things'. Her net annual worth is now estimated at US$250 million in revenue, with profit margins of 20 per cent. For her, failure is a positive. It is a step towards success:

> I think failure is nothing more than life's way of nudging you that you are off course. My attitude to failure is not attached to outcome, but in trying. It is liberating. Most people attach failure to something not working out or how people perceive you. This way, it is about answering to yourself.

She maintains that belief in gut instinct, in establishing something innovative, and never losing the belief that what you are doing is the key to thinking and dreaming big. She also says that for her, collaboration is the key to growth.

Thinking big? Then make the decisions big

> *I dare you to think bigger, to act bigger, and to be bigger, and I promise you a richer and more exciting life if you do.*
>
> — William Danforth, founder of Ralston-Purina,
> co-author of *I Dare You!*

Big vision requires the ability to make decisions — decisions about who you are going to be, how you are going to manage your mindset and your own belief system, and of course decisions about the future you want and making the decisive actions to get there.

Thinking bigger requires the ability to think on a global level, not just a local one. This is where the value of collaborative business and the team thought process comes in. Thinking creatively, flexibly, critically — all of these processes are easier when you are surrounded by people who are engaged and expert in what they do. If they are with you on the journey and also willing to think outside the box — what an absolute gift.

But it also depends on you and your ability to:

- make decisions on a daily basis
- plan
- set objectives
- realise your capacity to provide value to others within a business relationship
- overcome obstacles and challenges.

Those who think big choose not to listen to the dream stealers. They surround themselves with others who think big, they have a dream team of supporters and they work collaboratively, feeding the vision, creatively executing plan after plan, step after step in the journey to achieve that vision. They value positivity; they embrace belief and with this come focus, resilience and an innate ability to relentlessly pursue the dream.

Big thinkers:

- take big risks
- make bold decisions on a daily basis that others may not openly support
- are independent thinkers, and for that reason are prepared to accept those naysayers and not hesitate in those risky, big, bold decisions.

Take calculated risks

Just because you are a big thinker and you're taking risks, it doesn't make you a lunatic. This is not 'let's just see what happens'. Think about this maxim: thought before action. Of course sometimes there has to be a fly-by-the-seat-of-your-pants decision — but there is always an element of care, because you are so clear and focused on the big-picture vision and you involve a team of thought leaders in your dreams.

Lights, camera, action

Those who cultivate the habit of thinking big but do not act are only dreamers. To think big you must:

- act big
- take action
- step into your own unique spotlight
- use your voice
- be decisive moving towards your goals and objectives.

The discomfort zone

For those who think big, the comfort zone is not comfortable at all. The ones that are changing the game are:

- restless
- continually evolving and developing their thinking
- exploring ideas with others
- watching what is happening around them with the lens of their own dream.

Staying in the comfort zone is akin to staying in the Me space. Part of being in the We space is all about challenging yourself to do better, be better, think more, achieve more — and all within the framework of achieving with others. It isn't about going beyond capabilities — but it is about finding out just how your capabilities stretch, how to be bigger and better than you are, surrounding yourself with other experts that can add to your thinking, support your goals and make dreams come true.

Be alert and alarmed

Time frames are incredibly important when it comes to achieving those big dreams. If we don't set ourselves truly challenging — but achievable — time frames, the dream stays just that — a dream. Again, this is an area where a team is vital, as having others to push you when a vision may falter can be critical to success.

There is no I in...

This is the crux of thinking big. It is evident in the case studies presented, and in the whole concept of We space. Big thinkers associate with other big thinkers who are ambitious, motivated and inspire others to think bigger, act bigger and become bigger than they ever imagined possible. Steve Jobs may have been the first brick in the wall of the rejuvenated Apple, but as has been clearly shown after his death, the wall of its success is firmly still under construction.

Perhaps the biggest point to bear in mind when thinking big, and setting out to make decisions, is summed up in a quote from Michelle Obama. 'You can't make decisions based on fear and the possibility of what might happen.'

Richard Branson could be working in a travel agency in South Kensington. Mark Zuckerberg, a programmer at Microsoft. The point is, they swallowed their fear — and made bold decisions.

That's thinking bigger.

Case study — thinking bigger

Lisa Messenger has a history of practising 'thinking bigger', launching The Messenger Group in 2001. Starting life initially as a sponsorship agency, it rapidly evolved into a custom print and publishing house — with a twist. Her first self-published book, *Happiness*, clearly illustrated for her the value of building brands *and* people, and The Messenger Group business model of integrating marketing and custom publishing was born.

Ten years after launching The Messenger Group, Lisa realised she had reached a 'So, is this all there is?' moment in her business life; she had success, achievements and acclaim — but was that enough? All her working life, she had thought outside the square and sought to be an innovator, an inventor and a leader of the pack; now, all she felt was complacency. So what next?

Thinking (much) bigger is a natural philosophy for Lisa. 'Opportunity is around us every day and everywhere … Being nimble, flexible and willing to listen,' she says, is the key.

Enter a bright idea — shake up the stagnant Australian print magazine sector. It was in free-fall decline, and digital was on the rise. Journalists were being laid off left, right and centre. One of Australia's leading women's monthly publications, *Madison*, had unceremoniously just closed, despite having one of the industry's most experienced editors at the helm, and *Grazia*, the popular UK weekly clone, had also closed its doors. So what better time to think big and open a new magazine, with no knowledge of print layouts, deadlines, advertising campaigns … you name it, she was new to it.

But, as Lisa herself shares, 'naivety is often a huge advantage'; it drives you to seek advice, call on experts, surround yourself with excellence and push yourself way past your comfort zone. Her conversations with her own mentors and within her own circle of excellence drove her to think big, and play hard.

Lisa saw this unsettled market not as a cold, closed-off option, but rather as an opportunity to disrupt. This was a woman who knew that her success lay with her gut instinct; that a chance to challenge the status quo, change the landscape and create a multi-levelled and integrated product that was bigger, better and more aligned to consumer expectation than the current offerings on the shelves was her to a tee.

This was an opportunity for her to employ her knowledge, experience and contacts from 10 years of building The Messenger Group. She could not only create new content but, if she worked strategically in a commercially collaborative way with key influencers, opinion makers and thought leaders, she could innovate within an established industry to create a new product, with an accompanying unique model for marketing, sales and distribution.

She had a brave and bold focus: the magazine as a product, a brand unto itself, rather than a part of a traditional industry and thus bound by that industry's rules and measured against other publications. This is possibly the reason for her success; she has removed the barriers to traditional 'that's not the way it's done' thinking and instead seen the inherent potential of a good-looking, good-*thinking* commodity.

As Lisa states, 'I [had] never wanted to limit myself. So many people are fearful and hold themselves back. They have vision but they do nothing about it'.

She knew if she was going to make an impact she had to not only play with the big boys, but also play better and smarter than them—and that meant creating a big impact from the start. That could only come from backing herself 100 per cent:

> There is no normal to what we are doing. We're making it up as we go and just believing anything is possible every single step of the way. It's also about being authentic and having a very pure vision and intention—mine is to be the greatest resource for entrepreneurs on the planet, empowering them with the belief that anything is possible. I purposefully live my life by [this] example.

She collaborated with her extensive contact base to provide content, exclusive access to individuals and to open doors for advertising and partnership support. She reverse-engineered the advertising model by building relationships and engaging corporate support *first*, from the likes of Qantas, PwC and the Commonwealth Bank of Australia, with other advertisers quickly following in their steps. She engaged her loyal tribe of online supporters and personal contacts from day one to support the launch, share the news and engage others to purchase, driving significant brand exposure and distribution as well as realising a future market for the magazine.

Against all traditional business models and advice, Messenger launched her high-end magazine, *The Renegade Collective*, in 2013. The title describes itself as 'interviewing the people making the greatest impact in the business world, in any given industry; the game changers, the thought leaders, the rule breakers, the style makers'.

In other words, it's not about the what; it's about the who and the why. And it's about who is disrupting things on a global and a national level, and why they are doing it—whether it be in business, film, literature or science, you name it, Lisa is going to let you read all about it. Because she is the essence of what it means to think bigger.

Her first issue featured interviews and profiles of change-makers in the business world. With an initial print run of 100000 copies, this bi-monthly publication quickly became a monthly release, and within 13 months was distributed across 30 countries. *The Renegade Collective* has featured a plethora of interviews from eclectic sources, with entrepreneur extraordinaire Martha Stewart, actor John Cleese, designer Akira Isogawa, philanthropist Daniel Flynn and blogger Rumi Neely all featuring. With a supporting platform of other revenue drivers to leverage the traditional print model into an interactive multimedia experience for her loyal reader base, there is no doubt that Lisa Messenger is an example of thinking bigger, and the power of shifting from a space of Me to the collaborative magic of We. It is the Messenger *Group* for a reason, just as the magazine is called *The Renegade Collective* for more reasons than 'it sounds like something I would buy'.

There is no doubt her first year of success will beat steadily into the future. Her vision has been global from the moment she looked to the shelves of the local newsagent. Becoming a leader in her own space, breaking open a closed sector, planning for the future—this future-proofing will not only continue, it will become a part of business modelling, the collaborative effects of disrupting the norm. Because, in Lisa's own words, 'The vision for the future is to be the most influential entrepreneurial movement on the planet. It will be very multifaceted with the print magazine being just one pillar'.

Perhaps that's why her name is Messenger.

Case study—a true meeting of minds

For Adrian Morgan and Hish Fernando, a chance conversation about how many beaches Australia actually has led to a lifelong dream coming true for Adrian and a chance for Hish to use his entrepreneurial skills to facilitate that dream.

Picture the Coast is a partly crowd-funded endeavour to photograph—continuously—the entire Australian coastline by yacht, something that has never been done before. Skippered by Adrian, the voyage is expected to take six months, and the end result will be a panoramic picture of our incredible coast—hopefully on display at the MCG on the AFL Grand Final Day. It's something that has captured the public imagination, and also the eye of several high-profile personalities, including former Wallabies captain Stirling Mortlock, who is now the official Picture the Coast Ambassador, and people around the country who are dipping into their pockets to be a part of the adventure.

What is fascinating about this as a business proposition is the spirit of collaboration between the two partners. Their frank and open method of working together is a sign of the shift being seen from closed traditional methods into the realm of We entrepreneurialism, where they share responsibilities yet still have firm concepts of which areas of the vision they own.

For Hish, his strength clearly lies in organising the finance, the structure, the terms of the deal, whereas Adrian looks after the 'creative' side of the business; as Adrian puts it, 'Hish is the "off the boat" stuff, I'm the "on-board" stuff'. Hish, who is a partner at Charter during the day, and Adrian, an IT consultant for a telco, are very aware of boundaries and making sure they check in with each other and what they are doing in their own areas of expertise. This ensures no toes are trodden on and each is clear on the current path.

With a venture like this, which is breaking new ground, there is a large element of risk, and leaps of faith have to be taken—already they have seen that some things fail, and they have had to simply bite the business model bullet and move on. Because budgets are limited, things such as social media are in the hands of 'whoever has the time', for example, and this means promotional opportunities are often lost. But this does not mean there are regrets about not having a corporate machine behind them.

Sponsorship has been something they have been at pains to keep focused on the actual message of the voyage; so they have been very much seeking out companies that are like-minded in their attitude towards doing business collaboratively and openly. This has meant some lost chances, but it has also meant that the companies backing them fit with their own ethical stance and personal standards. They are companies that very much embrace the ethos of 'think bigger'.

Here are Hish and Adrian's views on what collaboration means to them with respect to business in general—and on this journey—from their own perspective, and in their own words:

> When you think about it, all businesses rely on commercial collaboration. The interaction between suppliers, oneself and the customer are all forms of collaboration—if done correctly. The relationship a business has with its customers is very special and privileged, and collaboration comes about through feedback and that relationship—now most evident through social media.

If we start looking at B2B interactions, collaboration comes from the supply of goods in a mutually beneficial way. The relationship requires two businesses, each maintaining a level of profitability to ensure long-term sustainability. The more collaboration in this negotiated position the better, and in a truly sustainable business model, both the supplier and the business realise there is benefit in long-term sustainability. In game theory terms, this is 'non-zero-sum' mechanics—there is money out there in the hands of the consumer and you both get some by *both* succeeding.

Continuing on the game theory for a moment, one of the challenges within business is that people tend to think of themselves in competition for the largest share—that if I get more, I have 'won'. This is true in a competitive environment, but in a collaborative environment it often comes out through 'imperfect information'—that is, keeping secrets. So this brings about the next notion of commercial collaboration—trust. Trust between partners, suppliers and customers. Again, the internet is a major force here. Trust is built using blogs and your social media presence, and the trust of people is a hard thing to gain but an easy thing to lose.

So commercial collaboration requires trust, and the explicit knowledge that everyone has to win for something to be successful. Again there are challenges with suppliers as often they are also supplying to our competitors, which raises doubts in the minds of who one can trust. This is often where we identify 'politics' and the power games that get in the way of collaboration.

So, summing that all up, commercial collaboration means:

- each participant gains a fair and equitable stake in the outcome
- there is a strong degree of trust in the relations and no 'imperfect information'
- politics stay firmly out of the relationship.

Within Picture the Coast we are working with a number of organisations to really understand where we can fit into their business, and why collaboration would be beneficial to them as well as us. We want to ensure that what we create benefits our partners, as well as the broader community. This project came about because of a vision to create the longest panorama showing the entire Australian coastline, so that all of Australia could then see our entire coastline. The project has a very clear education focus to the community and the world about how truly beautiful the Australian coast is. Our goal is that both our partners and the community see the benefit of this and contribute. To us, this represents a model of sustainable business, which we can then use to develop other projects, leveraging our trust and brand, and that of our partners for further success.

To date, we have formed partnerships (formal and informal) with the Lego Foundation, GigaPan, Deakin University, Green SuperCamp and several media partners. We are in discussions with stadiums around Australia to display the continuous image and Tourism Australia to support destination marketing exercises. We are working with Deakin University to support the study of Social Enterprises and Environmental Studies.

Ultimately, this venture is about capturing one of Australia's greatest assets: its coastline. And in doing so, we can contribute to the export economies we have including tourism, education and technical applications.

Capturing the picture is not about any of the individuals involved in the journey. It is in fact for everyone else, and therefore about everyone else.

Checklist — ReConnect Principle 6: Think bigger

You have the product. You have the vision. You have the business plan in place. You are already successful on so many levels — this is just another chapter. But it means disruption. It means evolution. It means risk-taking, a chance of failure. It means a complete leap of faith — in yourself, in your ability, and most importantly in your team's ability. This is an exercise in trust, because you are collaborating on a dream. And part of that trust means knowing when to stop dreaming and strategising and debating, and instead making that dream a reality. Those who have had the most success in thinking big will tell you that a large part of that success comes from the 'release' — and that has to come not at the 100 per cent mark, but at the '80 per cent means go' point. Decision-making is just as important to the 'think bigger' process as the dream.

☑ Are you willing to change your current situation?

☑ Do you understand what your fears are?

☑ Do you know what you need to do to use them constructively?

☑ What have you learned from your mistakes?

☑ Are you continually evolving your thinking?

☑ Are you ready to make decisions?

☑ Are you willing to embrace change?

☑ Are you surrounding yourself with other big thinkers?

☑ Do you want to innovate rather than perfect?

☑ Are you willing to disrupt?

☑ Are you walking the walk of thinking bigger?

chapter 12

ReConnect Principle 7 — Sponsor others

> Before you are a leader, success is all about growing yourself. When you become a leader, success is all about growing others.
>
> — *Jack Welch, former chairman and CEO of General Electric*

Sponsorship is so much more than mentoring. It is the intentional support of another, taking action, collaborating and sharing what you know and who you know to better someone else.

Sponsorship in the workplace, especially for women, is still regarded with a mixture of suspicion and ignorance — and a feeling of 'what's in it for me?' from the sponsor, which to a large extent colours the relationship before it even starts. For a truly two-way sponsorship to work, then, it has to happen in the right environment — and that environment is one of collaborative thinking.

Sponsors vs mentors

Sylvia Ann Hewlet, president and CEO of the Center for Talent Innovation and a Manhattan-based think tank says, 'Mentors advise, sponsors act'. And herein lies the subtle and yet crucial difference between mentors and sponsors.

On the one hand, mentors provide guidance, helping define visions and goals. Mentoring is more of a softly, softly approach; catching up for chats and being a willing sounding board for thoughts and ideas. Mentoring is more about giving advice and listening to concerns than saying, 'Yes, I will help you gain X'.

Active sponsorship, meanwhile, is far more powerful and a large obligation — but the results for those being sponsored are often far greater than for those being mentored. Usually sponsorship is from someone senior within the protégé's own company, or a successful entrepreneur within the same field. Fundamentally, sponsorship involves the active support of another to achieve your goals. Sponsors do the following:

- take action
- open doors
- make invaluable introductions
- give business/career leads
- are in it for the long haul
- help pave the path to success
- help others to achieve their visions, goals and dreams for personal and business success
- help build a powerful and diverse network
- influence activity and decision-making
- actively build the pipeline of future game changers, entrepreneurs, leaders and business owners.

Sponsorship takes collaboration to a whole new level, and this is why it is the seventh ReConnect Principle. Sponsorship does not necessarily have an immediate benefit to the sponsor, but it does do the following:

- build and support the next generation of leaders (men and women)

- show through behaviour modelling the requirements of future leaders

- share knowledge, insight and connection for the long-term benefit of the recipient.

Sponsorship as part of the We economy

What does sponsorship mean in terms of what it brings to a sponsor and a protégé?

To look at it purely from a selfish perspective, it increases the sponsor's worth. By actively supporting someone likely to be a future leader, as Anna Beninger, senior research analyst for Catalyst, explains:

> [You will find] that paying it forward pays back. Developing others really increases your own visibility... essentially what you are doing is showing the company that you are not only about your own advancement, but that you are invested in the future of the organisation.

What then happens makes this more altruistic than it may at first appear, because a domino effect begins, as it has been proven that people who are sponsored are more likely to sponsor others.

A 2011 study from the Center for Work-Life Policy published by the *Harvard Business Review* found that sponsorship can result in as much as a 30 per cent increase in promotions, pay rises and stretch assignments for a protégé.

Yet in spite of these clear advantages, the Catalyst study 'The Leadership Gap' found that many women are unaware of these benefits and lack allies among company leadership. In fact, 77 per cent of women were reported to believe that hard work and long hours, rather than connections, are responsible for advancement. The concern is, of course, that they are unaware of valuable connections that could be available to them.

From a young age, men are inducted into the world of sponsorship through their involvement in sports and clubs. Some men have access to an old boys' school alumni network, which provides encouragement and a leg up to those identified as having talent in some shape or form. And when men enter the business world, the active sponsoring continues, with mentoring very quickly progressing to 'Why don't you join me on the golf course this weekend?' In the past, women quite simply have not had access to this form of shortcut through the ranks because the women haven't been there to sponsor each other, and generally men haven't even considered it as an option, given the tendency to sponsor people such as ourselves. In its place, the focus has been mentoring.

Commercial collaboration requires a change to this established norm. The uncertain future is asking us to embrace diversity to future-proof our businesses, leaders and careers. Breaking through the old boys' network is never going to be easy, but collaboratively we can work towards a resolution. Sowing the seeds of sponsorship is a critical part of being present in the space of We and needs to become more of a focus across the corporate arena and entrepreneurial circles. Sylvia Ann Hewlet says that sponsors:

> ...make you visible to leaders within the company—and to top people outside as well. They connect you to career opportunities and provide air cover when you encounter trouble. When it comes to opening doors, they don't stop with one promotion. They'll see you to the threshold of power.

If we are to future-proof our leaders, business success and personal success, active sponsorship becomes an imperative. The collaborative We space delivers learning experiences, the chance to grow, and the opportunity to promote and sponsor others.

The business case for sponsoring others is there. Research conducted by the Center of Talent and Innovation found that those men and women who were sponsored felt that they were progressing through the ranks of business at a satisfactory pace — 70 per cent for men and 68 per cent for women, compared to 57 per cent of those individuals who did not have sponsors.

The Catalyst study highlights businesses that have instituted formal programs charged with training a diverse group of high-performing employees in the benefits of sponsorship.

According to the study, model programs can be found at McDonald's, Deutsche Bank, CH2M HILL and Citi. The Harvard study also applauded several companies with active sponsorship programs, including American Express, Cisco, Deloitte and Time Warner.

Procter & Gamble (P&G) has historically had a strong focus on diversity and inclusion. The company has a myriad strategies, programs and activities to support its employees and embrace inclusion across locations. P&G leaders have found that women in particular may have fewer role models, especially in areas such as technology or research and development. To address this issue, the company formed several core teams of senior women within business lines and aimed to support women on their career journey in these key fields. Many regional efforts, such as those in China and across Asia, link to broader corporate activities.

For those who are looking to sponsor, there needs to be an understanding of the following points:

- the time commitment involved; it's about giving of oneself and sharing knowledge and resources
- that they will have to advocate on their protégé's behalf, connecting them to important players and assignments
- that as a sponsor, they will not only give advice and listen; they will actively seek opportunities for advancement for their protégés.

For those wishing to be sponsored, there are important points to bear in mind too:

- This is a two-way street; stellar performance is expected because your sponsor is going to go the extra mile for you in terms of promoting you to influential people.

- Your sponsor is, without being cynical, looking for some kind of return on their investment.

- You have to make your sponsor look good, because they are endorsing you to a very high degree.

As Kerrie Peraino, Global Head of Talent at American Express, says:

> Trust is at the heart of this relationship...when I put my faith in up-and-coming talent and become their sponsor, I need to know I can totally depend on them—because they are, after all, walking around with my brand on.

And that is possibly the biggest benefit to both parties with sponsoring. The person being sponsored gets practical *help*, not just advice, in terms of their career advancement — and the person sponsoring has a talented individual at their fingertips, with the potential to become a valuable resource in their own arena, business or future collaborations.

Sponsorship isn't restricted to the corporate arena. Sometimes the biggest success stories come from a pairing between the business, entrepreneurial and outside world — and this is where the collaborative and the commercial mindsets really do come together. An example of this is giving circles, which are growing in popularity in the Asia-Pacific region, particularly in the South-East Asia region and in Australia itself. They are based on the US and Canadian model whereby groups of individuals — mainly entrepreneurs — donate their own money or time to a pooled fund, deciding together to give to several charity or community projects rather than a single entity and, in doing so, seeking to increase their awareness of and engagement in the issues covered by these charity or community projects. It leads to wider engagement over a larger number of issues and also a greater coverage of needs.

The First Seeds Fund is a singular achievement for its founders in Australia. It is based on a US giving circle and, in addition to donating their money, members also contribute their time and skills to support local causes. For First Seeds, their concentration is on giving back at a grassroots level to women and children in neglected communities in urban Australia, such as Warwick Farm, just outside of Sydney. Three generations of unemployment, child prostitution and lack of formal education had previously made this a 'forgotten community'; now, with the guidance of strong community leaders, First Seeds is making a tangible difference.

Part of what First Seeds does incredibly well is sponsor young women and girls in starting their own businesses and selling the resulting products at local markets. Every aspect of the business is covered — marketing, business plans, budgeting, design — in order to teach essential skills to girls who otherwise would have absolutely no exposure to any kind of mentoring or future-proofing.

A laser-sharp focus on sponsorship

Sponsorship, whether within the corporate environment, as an entrepreneur or in a philanthropic capacity, is a serious undertaking. Sponsorship does the following:

- requires an active collaborative attitude where talent fosters talent rather than like fosters like

- encourages a commitment to evolutionary learning, sharing knowledge and insight and actively opening doors and making those all-important introductions to drive commercial success for another

- involves commitment on a long-term basis and it will reflect not only on the protégé but also on the sponsor's reputation

- provides a two-way investment for both parties
- provides future-proofing success for the protégé but also ensuring higher visibility for the sponsor
- encourages actively pursuing your goals and enabling others to pursue theirs, which means it is a truly engaged collaborative relationship and provides a value exchange for both parties.

Essentially, the final and seventh ReConnect Principle — Sponsor others — is about securing the present and ensuring that the pipeline of the future generation of business leaders, entrepreneurs and philanthropists is solid. It is about ensuring that the future leaders and pioneers have effective role models now, sharing all they have learned along the way and opening the book of their contact base. Fundamentally, that they see the power of working as We.

Case study—organic leadership

Megan Larsen is an inspiration to anyone who is not prepared to do things the 'cookie-cutter' way, or accept things as being good enough simply because that's the way they have always been. Her pioneering approach to chemical-free skincare has paid dividends, with her 'chemical-free' brand, Sodashi, stocked in luxury hotels and spas across the globe.

Megan is a huge believer in the value of giving back, and sponsoring and mentoring employees and staff members as well as others who she feels have a flair for the industry is of vital importance to her. She embodies the true spirit of commercial collaboration, and ReConnect Principle 7 — Sponsor others, in that she has sponsored up-and-coming people who will one day be competitors—knowing that this will only enrich the industry and drive her on to further innovation.

This is Megan's story:

I've always been passionate about natural therapies, health and wellbeing. It's this passion that has underpinned my own personal success and the global success of Sodashi, and why I love to encourage and draw out the passions of others!

Sodashi was born from pure passion—a desire to provide an exceptional skin care product that would really work, be joyous to use and include the amazing goodness of nature. I was inspired after spending time in Provence, in the south of France, studying advanced aromatherapy and because I had spent so many years (and dollars) trying to find the perfect products for my sensitive skin. I wanted to create products that would be balancing, nurturing and anti-ageing for the skin. It all began on my kitchen bench and at the time the natural health store I owned was the perfect platform for me to sell the products and get feedback. Quickly the demand became overwhelming and my home-made skin-care products flew off the shelf. My first batch of 50 moisturisers lasted just three and a half days!

From the start, I've done things quite differently at Sodashi, being a pioneer in the chemical-free skin care and spa industry that delivers exceptional results. And importantly, from the start I've focused on investing in people first. After all, it's a team that builds a brand.

I went on to inspire a change in the global spa industry, educating people about the benefits of chemical-free skincare. I was a pioneer at the time, breaking down barriers about the efficacy of therapeutic-grade natural skin care products in the spa industry. Sodashi products are now available in over 70 luxury hotels, resorts and stand-alone spas, in 25 countries globally, including the prestigious Four Seasons George V in Paris, Emirates Wolgan Valley Resort & Spa in NSW and The Landmark Mandarin Oriental in Hong Kong.

But being a game changer is not always easy. You have to know how to deal with adversity, as things don't always go your way!

I learnt to deal with adversity from an early age. I grew up in New Zealand in a single-parent family and watched my mother set up a pottery business and turn it into a financially successful venture to support us. At a young age I observed how her positive mind brought a positive outcome in many challenging business situations and that has helped me so many times in my own business career.

The driving force in the success of Sodashi however has always been our people and why I am committed to investing in people first. I believe the health and wellbeing of each individual team member is paramount to having an engaged and dynamic team to move the business forward.

Over the past 14 years I have financially supported over 40 employees to learn transcendental meditation, giving them a tool to remove stress. This has been fundamental to creating a collaborative, caring and cohesive work environment. We have group meditation at the office every afternoon.

I've shared my passions of natural health and wellbeing, using outside consultants to inspire with their knowledge and engaging a resident Bowen therapist who provides the opportunity for each person to book their own personal treatment.

Not only do I find supporting the growth and development of others heartwarming, but it also encourages passion both professionally and personally and provides a wonderful working environment. The ultimate reward is to see people achieve their own potential and develop their own greatness.

I also believe the growth of the business is closely aligned to my own personal growth. A deep understanding of myself allows me to understand others.

I value my ability to work with highly creative individuals that can excel in their own brilliance. Trusting is vital, but also using my innate ability to guide others without constricting, taking the time to care and listen, and also giving and sharing with others the tools and experience to help them succeed and reach their own potential.

Someone once told me I have an eye for talent. An example of that is a staff member that came to work for me at the age of 19 as the company's third employee. She had first been inspired to work with me after listening to a presentation I gave at her beauty therapy school. For me the responsibility of employing someone so young, that potentially you would influence their whole career, never left me. After she showed great initiative as an administration assistant, I appointed her as the company's international spa trainer. She travelled the world training spa teams and together we developed Sodashi's world-class training program. Some years later I offered her the position as Sodashi's general manager, which she accepted. She went on to manage the company's day-to-day operations for over five years.

My own commitment to personal growth and learning means I've had many people in my life who inspire and motivate me. I've also been very lucky to have had a range of inspiring and supportive mentors during the company's evolution to date, and I now find myself mentoring others more and more, which I love to do!

I worked with Kim Morrison to launch her brand, Twenty8 — a range of aromatherapy and skincare products — and it was an invaluable experience for me. It was evident from the beginning that Kim's energy and enthusiasm for natural skincare echoed my own. Working with others to help them support and develop their businesses is such a joy for me, and in helping others I have learnt so much more about myself.

Being acknowledged as an 'inspiration and mentor' to Zoe Foster Blake on her journey to launching her own product range was also a great privilege. It has been wonderfully enriching, exchanging insights and knowledge with such a dynamic player in the beauty industry.

Ultimately, in putting people—your employees, your peers, your colleagues—first, I believe you generate a highly engaged and motivating community that can't help but create success. It's about future-proofing your business by paying it forward.

And of course I continue to have tough days, but I learn more and more that often these are about collecting the strength and energy for what's coming next.

I dare people to think blue sky. It is possible; anything is possible that you really put your mind to and dig deep for. Fifteen years ago I could never have imagined Sodashi's global success today. Dare to be a game changer and a thought leader, and don't be scared to break rules!

Case study—making a difference one person at a time

For Kate Sutton, founder of UberKate Jewellery, being involved with the First Seeds Fund was a completely new experience. She had never actively mentored or sponsored anyone previously, despite nurturing talent in her workshop on a staff level. UberKate is an internationally successful brand, worn by celebrities around the world, as well as by Australian women from Perth to Penrith.

This is Kate's story of how important sponsoring can be in making a difference to 'just one' person at a time, and in terms of collaborative ways of working:

I started my sponsoring journey last year, when I received an invitation as part of a group from the First Seeds Fund to go to a high school in Sydney's outer south-west and teach a group of year 11 female students about jewellery making, and to basically look further for their futures, to see there were more opportunities out there than just working in the local fish and chip shop or going on unemployment benefits—if they were willing to look outside the box.

To be honest, my first visit there left me not only taken aback, but very shocked; there were only four girls present in the class, with no real discipline. It started off extremely rocky, and my whole plan for what I was going to take them through was thrown out the window, because I could see that they weren't ready for it and weren't going to listen.

But then, once I had unpacked all the beads and jewellery-making kit out on the table, and started to talk…there was a turnaround. Interest picked up, and over the unpacking, the girls started to talk. They explained their lives. I watched these girls, some with scars on their wrists from failed self-harm attempts, talk about the unhappiness in their families, the feeling that the future they wanted was 'never going to happen' because of their circumstances. I saw a sisterhood emerging. This was when I saw just what my sponsoring would mean to these girls, and what it was beginning to mean to me.

Watching the girls piling bangles up, making them for friends and family, and seeing others becoming involved, uplifted me. For people like me at a certain level in business, and with a busy family, to step outside and mentor, to be able to inspire just one girl—this was something I wanted and needed to do.

I was invited after this initial workshop course to graduation. The girls I had mentored were styled by other First Seeds participants and dressed up, and did a runway show. To see the transformation in them—to see what I saw from beginning to end, that incredible difference in confidence, just from some self-belief and promotion—they were ready to take on the world. There were many dreams that had evolved with the First Seeds program—including a would-be journalist running around interviewing everyone.

For me, my sponsorship journey culminated in a girl called Jasmine, whom I connected with during the beading workshop. I became her one-on-one sponsor—taking her on beading selection trips, teaching her about purchasing and marketing, setting up a business plan, and helping her create her own jewellery in the school library. Jasmine brought her own culture into the jewellery; she wears the hijab, and is very traditional and very unassuming. So I set her a very tough challenge: having a market stall on International Women's Day at Warwick Farm. This was in conjunction with CBA Women in Focus. She made over $340. Her mum, who was also previously incredibly quiet and uninvolved, saw what was happening for her daughter; that this wasn't just about purchasing and stringing some beads together, that it was about a future, a viable opportunity. She ended up getting very involved on the business management side—or she will be, once Jasmine finishes her HSC.

Previous to this experience, I had struggled with sponsoring as I was concerned about over-committing—I had my own business, children, staff, and I felt if I half-did anything I would let everyone, including a protégé, down. This time I had the time and energy.

For all women out there, entrepreneurs and corporate leaders alike—if you only make a difference with one person—imagine the chain! I will definitely do it again. This time, I will work with someone who is ready to go, go, go—perhaps someone with young children, or an adult who is ready to work in the field full time. But help just one person and the flow-on effect is enormous. Make a difference, and collaborate. It will push you on to new ideas in your own business.

Checklist — ReConnect Principle 7: Sponsor others

Sponsoring others is a critical part of the commercial collaboration process — an engaged and active two-way investment of skills, connections and knowledge, a value exchange to future-proof both parties.

☑ Do you have a sponsor?

☑ Who are you sponsoring?

☑ Are you actively sharing knowledge and connections, opening doors of opportunity for others?

☑ Are you enabling others to pursue their goals and dreams as well as pursuing your own?

☑ What is the value exchange of your sponsorship collaboration?

☑ Is the nature of your sponsorship open and diverse — are you sponsoring against type, against inbuilt prejudices, against sex?

Conclusion

Collaboration is key; it takes innovation and creativity to
the next room.

— *Shawn Lukas, designer and composer*

Employee Engagement: The state at which there is
reciprocal trust between the employee and leadership to
do what's right however, whenever and with whomever.

— *Dan Pontefract, author of* Flat Army

For some, the journey into the unknown future is not going to
be one of excitement and anticipation. There are always going
to be those among us who view the new and the unfamiliar
with trepidation and the kind of fear that can't be contained or
overcome. For them, the thought of commercial collaboration
is a huge part of the unknown — and a part of the fear.

For these individuals, looking inwards is always going to be the
default position. It is safe and secure and provides a zone of
neutrality when everything else is a whirlwind of volatility and
confusion.

As personalities, this is absolutely their right. As business
leaders — as thought leaders — it will be, and to some extent
already is, an untenable option, because the pace of change that
is happening on a global scale means they simply will not keep
up with those who are willing to look outside themselves, to
embrace the opinions, thoughts and ideas of others.

There are times when holding your cards close to your chest in business terms is absolutely a necessity. Confidentiality still has to be maintained with respect to intellectual property and resources. Commercial collaboration is not pie-in-the-sky, reveal-all, socialistic idealism — although it is sometimes perceived this way, particularly by large corporates that are suspicious of the concept of 'open engagement'. But being able to understand what collaboration actually means is something that those who are fearful will never grasp, because they believe only in the negative aspects of it.

Those who are willing to be a part of a collaborative working environment are doing so because they want to be challenged. They want the opportunity to constantly learn from others, and to share what they've learned. To engage on an intellectually challenging level with like-minded thinkers. To see their own business — or own business area — benefit from the knowledge of specialists. To be happy knowing that they are on the edge of technological advancement, constantly pushing the 'what if' button — because as a team, they feel secure enough to take risks. The concept of commercial collaboration and the move from the Me space to the We space and way of thinking is, as this book has shown, not something for the faint-hearted. It's for those who can see the far-reaching benefits of what the We space is about — and yes, it is a gradual move which involves challenging thinking. But it is not something that you have to contemplate in solitude.

Every part of the We space is done with the backing of others. Overcoming fear, facing up to vulnerability — it is done with full disclosure and honesty, in the knowledge that by sharing your fears, you are empowering not just yourself, but those who work with and for you. You are giving the *team* the opportunity for empowerment. You are giving the team the opportunity to trust.

When you disrupt the status quo, when you lead and disturb the accepted and the everyday, you are forging a new strength and getting rid of the weak and humdrum that bog down business decisions and keep the processes stale and stagnant. Again, this is happening in the spirit of openness and full disclosure. You are not moving secretively, but so that those in your team or circle of excellence are aware of your thought processes and why you are taking the actions you are. In this way, you have backup — and trust in your actions.

Understanding the power of your network and using its potential is intrinsic to the We mentality. To care about the wellbeing of those who are connected to you through business similarities, or ethical focus, or a desire to advance the same cause — and expecting nothing in return — this creates a fantastic opportunity for collaborative relationships, and also for a true value exchange, where 'what's in it for Me' turns into 'what can I do for you'.

Every single case study that has been presented within this book shows the same basic tenets: the ability to look to the long-term future. These are leaders who:

- are able to think big
- recognise the need to act as a team
- embrace fears and vulnerabilities
- see the value in helping others see their worth
- actively engage with others
- act with bravery
- promote irrespective of gender or age, based on merit
- are innovative
- disrupt the status quo
- lead with a questioning spirit
- see what commercial collaboration brings to an entrepreneurial mind.

These are leaders who do not accept the boring and the average simply because that has been acceptable in the past.

It is not enough, in the words of the amazing Sheryl Sandberg, to 'lean in' for future-proofing our success, our businesses and our careers. As leaders who are taking teams into an uncertain future it's now about leaning *out* and collaborating with others. Because to lean out means to embrace and engage on an unforeseen aggregated level — where thinking bigger than ever before will bring rewards to a collective commercial mind.

Make excellence a habit. Make communication a way of thinking. The We space is not a pipedream. There are businesses and leaders who are clearly succeeding by operating within this framework. It is the centre of discussion among academics, thought leaders and consulting groups. Those corporations and entrepreneurs who are using the space well, and understanding the shift in thinking, needed to get there. They are seeing procedures streamlined, the bottom line coming up, employees more engaged and happier. Their 'communities' are becoming communities without the inverted commas.

The message is clear.

Save Me for the mirror, and join the We space in the real world.

Other people give far more interesting answers than your own reflection.

Index

Learn more with practical advice from our experts

Stop Playing Safe
Margie Warrell

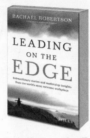

Leading on the Edge
Rachael Robertson

Lead with Wisdom
Mark Strom

The Social Executive
Dionne Kasian-Lew

The People Manager's Toolkit
Karen Gately

The New Rules of Management
Peter Cook

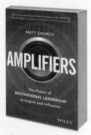

Amplifiers
Matt Church

Hooked
Gabrielle Dolan and
Yamini Naidu

The Ultimate Book of Influence
Chris Helder

Available in print and e-book formats

WILEY